How to use your Snap Rev

This 'Blood Brothers' Snap Revision Text Guide wi
AQA English Literature exam. It is divided into tw
find help for the bits you find tricky. This book co
know for the exam:

Plot: what happens in the play?

Setting and Context: what periods, places, events and attitudes are relevant to understanding the play?

Characters: who are the main characters, how are they presented, and how do they change?

Themes: what ideas does the author explore in the play, and how are they shown?

The Exam: what kinds of question will come up in your exam, and how can you get top marks?

To help you get ready for your exam, each two-page topic includes:

Key Quotations to Learn
Short quotations to memorise that will allow you to analyse in the exam and boost your grade.

Summary
A recap of the most important points covered in the topic.

Sample Analysis
An example of the kind of analysis that the examiner will be looking for.

Quick Test
A quick-fire test to check you can remember the main points from the topic.

Exam Practice
A short writing task so you can practise applying what you've covered in the topic.

Glossary
A handy list of words you will find useful when revising 'Blood Brothers' with easy-to-understand definitions.

AUTHOR:
PAUL BURNS

 ebook

To access the ebook version of this Snap Revision Text Guide, visit

collins.co.uk/ebooks
and follow the step-by-step instructions.

Published by Collins
An imprint of HarperCollins*Publishers*
1 London Bridge Street
London SE1 9GF

HarperCollins*Publishers*
1st Floor,Watermarque Building,
Ringsend Road
Dublin 4, Ireland

© HarperCollins*Publishers* Limited 2018

ISBN 9780008306625

First published 2018

10 9 8 7 6 5 4

British Library Cataloguing in Publication

Data.

A CIP record of this book is available from

the British Library.

Printed in UK by Ashford Colour Press Ltd.

Commissioning Editor: Gillian Bowman
Managing Editor: Craig Balfour
Author: Paul Burns
Proofreader: Jill Laidlaw
Project manager and editor:
  Project One Publishing Solutions, Scotland
Typesetting: Jouve
Cover designers: Kneath Associates and
  Sarah Duxbury
Production: Natalia Rebow

ACKNOWLEDGEMENTS

© Willy Russell, 2001, Blood Brothers,Methuen
Drama, an imprint of Bloomsbury Publishing Plc.

The author and publisher are grateful to
the copyright holders for permission to use
quoted materials and images.

Every effort has been made to trace copyright
holders and obtain their permission for the
use of copyright material. The author and
publisher will gladly receive information
enabling them to rectify any error or omission
in subsequent editions. All facts are correct at
time of going to press.

MIX
Paper from
responsible source
FSC
www.fsc.org **FSC™ C007454**

This book is produced from independently
certified FSC™ paper to ensure responsible
forest management.

For more information visit:
www.harpercollins.co.uk/green

Contents

Act 1 (part 1)

You must be able to: understand what happens at the beginning of the play.

What is the setting?

The play is set over a period of about 20 years, mainly in Liverpool and in a new town near the city.

How does the play begin?

The narrator introduces a re-enactment of the deaths of Mickey and Edward at the end of the play. Mrs Johnstone asks the audience to judge her part in the story and we go back to the beginning of the story.

Who are the characters?

Mrs Johnstone was married young, when pregnant. At 25 she 'looked like forty-two / with seven hungry mouths to feed'. When the action begins she has been abandoned by her husband, is pregnant again and cannot pay her bills.

Mrs Lyons employs Mrs Johnstone as a cleaner. She and her husband have not been able to have children and her husband is unwilling to adopt.

The narrator comments on the action and plays other parts, such as the milkman and the gynaecologist.

What changes the situation?

The gynaecologist tells Mrs Johnstone that she is expecting twins. Mrs Johnstone reveals to Mrs Lyons that 'the **Welfare**' have told her that she should put some of her children into care. She is worried that she will not manage with two more.

Mrs Lyon asks Mrs Johnstone to 'give one' to her when they are born. Her husband is working abroad and will not return until after the babies are due, so she will be able to pretend that she is pregnant and that the baby is theirs.

Mrs Johnstone is convinced by Mrs Lyons' description of the good life her child will have. She agrees. Mrs Lyons makes her swear on the Bible that she will keep the bargain.

What happens when the twins are born?

Mrs Lyons reminds Mrs Johnstone of their bargain. Mrs Johnstone tells her to take one of the twins. When Mrs Lyons has gone, she tells her other children that one of the twins has 'gone up to heaven'.

When Mrs Johnstone returns to work, she pays a lot of attention to the baby, making Mrs Lyons uneasy. Mrs Lyons sacks Mrs Johnstone and offers her money.

Mrs Johnstone refuses the money and tries to take the baby but Mrs Lyons stops her by making up a superstition – that when twins have been secretly parted, if either of them learns that he is a twin 'they shall both immediately die'. She says Mrs Johnstone must never tell anyone the truth. She gives the money to Mrs Johnstone, who takes it and leaves.

Key Quotations to Learn

NARRATOR: So did y'hear the story of the Johnstone twins? / As like each other as two new pins[...] / An' did you never hear how the Johnstones died, / Never knowing that they shared one name.

MRS JOHNSTONE: (*almost inaudibly*) Give one to me.

MRS LYONS: You won't tell anyone about this, Mrs Johnstone, because if you do, you will kill them.

Summary

- Mrs Johnstone has seven children and is pregnant with twins.
- Her employer, Mrs Lyons, is unable to have children but desperately wants a child.
- Mrs Johnstone agrees to give one of the twins to Mrs Lyons.
- Mrs Lyons tells Mrs Johnstone she must not tell anyone about what has happened.

Questions

QUICK TEST
1. How does the audience know what will happen at the end of the play?
2. What is the relationship between Mrs Johnstone and Mrs Lyons?
3. How do the two women seal their bargain?
4. What does Mrs Johnstone tell her children about the twin she has given away?

EXAM PRACTICE
Using at least one of the 'Key Quotations to Learn', write a paragraph analysing how Russell starts the play by sowing the seeds of an inevitable tragedy.

Act 1 (part 2)

You must be able to: understand what happens in the second half of Act 1.

When is the second half of Act 1 set?

The action moves on seven years to when the twins are 7 years old.

What happens when Mickey and Edward meet?

Mickey is upset about the way he is treated as the youngest in the family, especially by his brother Sammy.

He meets Edward for the first time. They discover that they were born on the same day and Mickey says they can be 'blood brothers'. They cut their hands and mix their blood. Mickey introduces Edward to Mrs Johnstone. When she sees him she chases him away and tells him not to come round again.

Mickey goes to Edward's house and asks if he can come out to play. Mrs Lyons will not let him and questions Edward about Mickey, telling him not to go near him. Upset, Edward swears at his mother, using a word Mickey has taught him. Mrs Lyons hits him and then gets upset.

How is Linda introduced?

Mickey and the other children, including Sammy and Linda, are seen playing a series of children's games, all of which end in violent 'death'. When Mickey swears at them, the other children tell him he will die and go to hell. Linda defends Mickey and comforts him when he gets upset about dying.

Mickey and Linda go to Edward's house and persuade him to go out to play with them. When Mrs Lyons comes to look for him in the garden and cannot find him she tells her husband she wants to move because she is frightened.

Mickey, Linda and Edward go to the park, where they use Sammy's air pistol to shoot at a statue of Peter Pan (the fictional character who never grows up). They are caught by a policeman.

How does Act 1 end?

The policeman visits Mrs Johnstone and warns her about her children's behaviour. He then visits Mr and Mrs Lyons. Mr Lyons tells Edward that they are going to move house.

Edward visits Mickey to say goodbye. Mrs Johnstone gives him a locket containing a picture of her and Mickey, telling him to keep it secret.

Mrs Johnstone gets a letter telling her that the family is going to be rehoused 'in the country'. The Act ends on a hopeful note as the Johnstones arrive at their new home.

Key Quotations to Learn

MICKEY: See this means that we're blood brothers, an' that we always have to stand by each other.

MRS JOHSTONE: Beat it, go home before the bogey man gets y'.

MRS LYON: It's just ... it's these people ... these people that Edward has started mixing with.

MRS JOHNSTONE: 'Ey, we'll be all right out here son, away from the muck an' the dirt an' the bloody trouble.

Summary

- Aged 7 Mickey and Eddie meet and become 'blood brothers' by cutting their hands.
- Both their mothers forbid them from seeing each other.
- Mickey introduces Eddie to his friend Linda, and they play together.
- The Lyons move away from the city, and the Johnstones are rehoused in a new town.

Questions

QUICK TEST
1. How do Mickey and Edward show that they are blood brothers?
2. How does Mrs Lyons react to finding out that Edward and Mickey are friends?
3. What does Mrs Johnstone give to Edward?
4. What does Mrs Johnstone feel about moving house?

EXAM PRACTICE
Using at least one of the 'Key Quotations to Learn', write a paragraph explaining how Russell presents the two mothers' reactions to their sons' friendship.

You must be able to: understand what happens in the first part of Act 2.

How does Act 2 start?

Mrs Johnstone sings about how life has improved for her since she moved to the new town, although Sammy has been in trouble with the law and is on the **dole**. All her children except him and Mickey have moved away. Mickey is now 14.

How do Mickey and Edward meet again?

While Mrs Johnstone teases Mickey about Linda and 'courting', Mrs Lyons teaches Edward to dance before he goes back to his boarding school.

On the way to school Linda tells Mickey she loves him, embarrassing him. Sammy threatens the bus conductor with a knife and steals his bag.

Meanwhile, Edward is suspended (excluded) from his private school because he will not give the teacher the locket which Mrs Johnstone gave him.

We see Linda and Mickey at their **secondary modern school**. Bored, Mickey gets into trouble with the teacher and Linda gets into trouble for defending him.

At home, Edward shows Mrs Lyons his locket. She recognises Mrs Johnstone but thinks Mickey is Edward. Edward refuses to tell her where he got the locket because 'it's a secret', making her upset and angry.

Out walking with Linda, Mickey sees Edward looking out of his window. Fed up with Mickey's attitude to her, Linda goes home. Edward approaches Mickey and they recognise each other.

What happens next?

Mickey takes Edward home to see Mrs Johnstone before Mickey and Edward go to see a pornographic film together.

Mrs Lyons has followed the boys and is waiting for Mrs Johnstone. She confronts her about the locket before offering her money to leave the area. When Mrs Johnstone refuses, she attacks her with a knife. Mrs Johnstone manages to overcome her and she goes, cursing Mrs Johnstone.

After the film, Mickey and Edward meet Linda, who is there with a friend. The three of them quickly become friends again and, as time passes, they spend a lot of time together.

Key Quotations to Learn

MRS JOHNSTONE: The house we got was lovely / The neighbours are a treat, / They sometimes fight on Saturday night, / But never in the week.

MICKEY (*speaking*): If I was like him / I'd know (*singing*) all the right words

NARRATOR: But leave them alone, let them go and play / They care not for what's at the end of the day.

Summary

- Mickey is now 14 and life is better for the Johnstones in their new home.
- Linda annoys Mickey by telling him that she loves him.
- The twins meet again for the first time since they left the city.
- After Edward is sent home from school, Mrs Lyons sees the locket.
- Mrs Lyons attacks Mrs Johnstone with a knife.
- Mickey, Edward and Linda enjoy spending a lot of time together as they age from 15 to 17.

Questions

QUICK TEST
1. How old are the twins at the start of Act 2?
2. What sort of school do Mickey and Linda attend?
3. Why is Edward suspended?
4. What does Mrs Lyons want Mrs Johnstone to do?

EXAM PRACTICE
Using at least one of the 'Key Quotations to Learn', write a paragraph explaining how Russell shows the developing relationships between Mickey, Edward and Linda in the first part of Act 2.

Act 2 (part 2)

You must be able to: understand what happens in the second part of Act 2.

How does the second half of Act 2 start?

The twins and Linda grow up from 15 to 18 years old.

How do the twins' lives change?

Edward goes away to university and Mickey asks Linda to go out with him. Linda becomes pregnant and they marry. Mickey loses his factory job as the firm makes redundancies.

When Edward returns for the Christmas holidays, he cannot understand Mickey's attitude to losing his job and, after Mickey refuses money that Edward offers him, they quarrel.

Edward, not knowing that Linda has married Mickey, tells her he loves her. At the same time Sammy offers Mickey £50 to act as a look-out for him during an armed robbery. Mickey agrees.

During the robbery Mickey shoots a man. He hides the gun in his mother's house and escapes before the police arrive. Mickey is arrested and sent to prison.

What happens next?

While in prison Mickey becomes depressed and dependent on pills. He is released before he has served his seven-year sentence.

Meanwhile, Edward has finished university and is now a local councillor.

In an effort to help Mickey recover, Linda helps to get him a job and finds a new house for them.

Mickey realises that she has been to Edward for help. She says she loves him and she wants him to stop taking anti-depressants.

While Mickey struggles to give up the pills, Linda becomes romantically involved with Edward. Mrs Lyons sees them together and tells Mickey. Angry, Mickey goes to his mother's house and gets the gun.

How does the play end?

At the Town Hall, Edward is making a speech when Mickey bursts in with the gun and confronts Edward about his relationship with Linda, saying she was the only thing he has left. Edward says that they are just friends.

Policemen enter and tell Mickey to put down the gun. Mrs Johnstone arrives and tells Mickey not to shoot Edward because 'he's your brother'. Mickey angrily asks why she did not give him away instead. The gun goes off and kills Edward. The policemen shoot and kill Mickey.

The closing **tableau** is the same as the one at the beginning of the play.

Key Quotations to Learn

Mickey is left alone, sitting dejected. We hear Christmas bells.

MICKEY: I could have been … I could have been him!

MRS JOHNSTONE: Tell me it's not true,

MRS JOHNSTONE: Say it's just a story.

Summary

- Mickey marries Linda, who is pregnant, but soon afterwards he loses his job.
- Sammy gets Mickey involved in an armed robbery and Mickey is sent to prison.
- When Mickey gets out, Linda asks Edward for help getting him a job and a house.
- When Mrs Lyons tells Mickey that Edward and Linda are seeing each other, Mickey gets the gun and goes after Edward.
- Mrs Johnstone tells Mickey and Edward that they are brothers.
- Mickey's gun goes off, killing Edward, and Mickey is killed by the police.

Questions

QUICK TEST
1. Where does Sammy hide the gun?
2. How does Edward help Mickey and Linda?
3. Who tells Mickey about Linda and Edward??
4. What does Mrs Johnstone tell Mickey at the end of the play?

EXAM PRACTICE
Using at least one of the 'Key Quotations to Learn', write a paragraph explaining how Russell builds the tension in the second half of Act 2.

Structure

You must be able to: understand the significance of the different ways Russell has structured the play.

How is the play organised?

The play is in two acts, with an interval.

Each act contains many short **scenes**. The set does not change and the action is continuous. Sometimes the scenes flow into each other; sometimes they are linked by the narrator's speeches or by songs.

What is the significance of the opening and closing scenes being the same?

By starting with a tableau of the dead twins, Russell removes any sense of mystery about how the play might end. Instead, he makes the audience curious about how and why that end comes about.

Apart from the beginning, the action unfolds in **chronological** order, following the twins' story from birth to death.

How is the rest of the play structured to keep the audience interested and create tension?

Immediately after the opening scene, the audience is introduced to Mrs Johnstone, learning about her circumstances and background. Through her, we then meet Mrs Lyons and learn about her situation. This part of a play is called the **exposition**.

The real action of the play starts when Mrs Johnstone decides to give one of her babies to Mrs Lyons. An event like this in a play or story is sometimes called the **inciting incident**. From now on, the characters' lives will change.

Tension is created when the babies are born as we wonder whether Mrs Johnstone will keep the bargain. An important **turning point** comes when the boys are aged 7 and meet each other. Mrs Lyons' discovery of their friendship creates more tension.

Although the first act ends on an optimistic note, lessening tension, the audience will sense the underlying **irony**, knowing that the play must end in tragedy.

After the beginning of Act 2 establishes the Johnstones' situation, tension is increased when the twins meet again. From here the pace of the action increases. A further important turning point occurs when Mickey marries Linda at the same time as he and others are shown losing their jobs. This leads to his getting involved in Sammy's crime, building to the **climax**, when he shoots Edward and is himself shot.

The narrator's speech and the final song lower the tension and give the audience an opportunity to reflect on what it has seen.

Key Quotations to Learn

The lights come up in a re-enactment of the final moments of the play – the deaths of MICKEY *and* EDWARD. (Act 1)

MRS JOHNSTONE: We're goin' away, / Oh, bright new day. *Curtain.* (Act 1)

COMPANY: Say you didn't mean it, / Say it's just the end / Of an old movie from years ago / Of an old movie with Marilyn Monroe. *Curtain.* (Act 2)

Summary

- The play begins as it will end, so the audience thinks not about what will happen but how and why it will happen.
- The play contains a lot of very short scenes; the action on stage is continuous.
- There are important turning points when the twins meet at 7- and 14-years old.
- From Mickey's involvement in the robbery in Act 2 the tension builds quickly towards the tragic climax.

Questions

QUICK TEST
1. How does the play begin?
2. Give two ways in which Russell links short scenes.
3. In what way is the optimistic ending of Act 1 ironic?
4. What happens at the climax of the play?

EXAM PRACTICE
Using at least one of the 'Key Quotations to Learn', write a paragraph explaining the effect on the audience of the ways in which Russell opens and closes the acts.

Willy Russell and *Blood Brothers*

You must be able to: understand how the play's meaning has been shaped by the author's life and the circumstances surrounding the writing of the play.

Who is Willy Russell?

Russell was born in 1947 in Whiston, just outside Liverpool, and grew up in rural Knowsley village. He left school at 15 with one 'O' level in English Language and became a ladies' hairdresser, an experience to which he partly attributes his success in writing female characters. He returned to education at the age of 20 and trained as a teacher.

How did he become a writer?

Russell became involved in folk music and wrote plays while at college. Director and writer John McGrath saw some of his work at the Edinburgh Festival and recommended him to the Liverpool Everyman, a theatre which was known at the time for plays on local themes and by local writers.

Russell's work for the Everyman included *John, Paul, George, Ringo and Bert*, a play with music about the Beatles (1974) and *Breezeblock Park* (1975), a comedy set in a Liverpool **council house**. Russell had huge success with *Educating Rita*, both as a play (1980) and a film (1983).

Why did Russell write *Blood Brothers*?

The original version of *Blood Brothers* was written for a company called Merseyside Young People's Theatre, which took plays written for children and young people to local schools. The play had five actors, no set and only one song. It was first performed in November 1981.

Russell developed this short play into a full scale **musical**, writing the music and **lyrics** himself, which was first performed at the Liverpool Playhouse in January 1983 before transferring to London. Since then it has been performed all over the world.

How has Willy Russell's background influenced the play?

Russell's experience of education is reflected in the rather negative view of it shown in the play.

Russell's childhood and his feeling that his life was turned round by his wife's steadier, more middle-class family, are reflected to some extent in the contrast between Mickey and Edward's families, although his background was very different from the Johnstones'.

In his work he identifies strongly with working-class characters, reflecting both his experiences growing up and the political and theatrical ideas he encountered in music and theatre in the 1970s.

How have the origins of the play influenced its style?

The play's focus on young characters growing up is a reflection of its original intended audience.

The simplicity of the story and the treatment of the themes also reflect the fact that the play was intended for a young audience.

The fluid nature of the action and the use of actors to play several parts reflect the style of the original play.

Summary

- Russell was born and grew up near Liverpool, leaving school at 15.
- He started writing plays while training to be a teacher.
- *Blood Brothers* was originally a short play, written to be performed in schools.
- Russell turned it into a musical, which was first performed in 1983.

Questions

QUICK TEST
1. Name two other plays by Willy Russell.
2. How does Russell think his first job influenced his writing?
3. What was the target audience of the original version of *Blood Brothers*?
4. How do the play's characters and themes reflect the original target audience?

EXAM PRACTICE
Look at this **dialogue** from Act 2 between Mickey and the teacher:
   MICKEY: It's borin'.
   TEACHER: Yes, yes, you might think it's boring but you won't be sayin' that when you can't get a job.
   MICKEY: Yeh. Yeh an' it'll really help me to get a job if I know what some soddin' pygmies in Africa have for their dinner!
Relating your ideas to the context, write a paragraph exploring how Russell presents ideas about education in *Blood Brothers*.

Folk Music and Musical Theatre

You must be able to: understand how the writer's methods have been shaped by the traditions of folk music and musical theatre.

What is folk music?

Traditional folk music is usually associated with a particular culture or region. Folk songs are often based on historical events or the lives of real people. They were not written down and their composers' names are not known.

'Contemporary folk' or 'folk revival' refers to music in a folk style coming out of the revival of interest in folk music during the mid-twentieth century.

How is folk music important in Russell's career?

During the 1960s there was a thriving folk music scene in Liverpool. Sea shanties, traditional sailors' songs, were often sung, as well as songs from other places, and original work. Poetry readings were also popular at this time.

Willy Russell performed semi-professionally in a folk group. He was especially interested in new folk songs that were being written on local themes.

How has folk music influenced *Blood Brothers*?

Russell has described the play as a 'folk opera'.

Like folk music, it tells a story about ordinary people. The events of the story, like those of many folk songs, are dramatic (perhaps even **melodramatic**), violent and emotional, but told with humour.

The songs – and the spoken verse – use simple, everyday language with strong simple **rhythm** and rhyme schemes, giving them power and making them easy to remember.

What is musical theatre?

The term 'musical theatre' is used to describe theatrical productions that include dialogue, songs and dance. However, some 'musicals' are like operas in having no spoken dialogue; others, like *Blood Brothers*, contain little or no dance.

Modern musicals developed in America in the early twentieth century from 'revues', which were light-hearted, comic entertainments. Writers began to place more importance on story and character. Musicals such as *Showboat, Oklahoma* and *West Side Story* explore serious and even tragic themes.

When Russell wrote *Blood Brothers* there was a revival of interest in musicals in Britain, with shows such as *Jesus Christ Superstar, Evita* and *Les Miserables* enjoying great success in London theatres.

How does *Blood Brothers* reflect the conventions of musical theatre?

Russell uses songs to explore the thoughts and emotions of his characters, sometimes in a comic way (as in 'I wish I was our Sammy') but more often to express strong emotions ('Say it's just a story'), which the characters might be unable to express in dialogue.

The songs can also help to move on the story ('The jury found him guilty') and to link scenes that are set in different places and at different times.

Like most musicals, *Blood Brothers* includes a **chorus** (a group of actors – see pages 36–37).

Although *Blood Brothers* has little dance content, it does use movement to convey feelings and advance the plot, for example in the sequence where the Johnstones move house at the end of Act 1.

 Summary

- Russell was influenced by traditional and contemporary folk music.
- Folk songs often tell dramatic and emotional stories about ordinary people.
- Modern musicals combine dialogue, music and dance to explore serious themes.
- *Blood Brothers* follows the conventions of musical theatre.

 Questions

QUICK TEST
1. What kind of folk music especially interested Russell?
2. What is the effect of the simple rhythm and rhyme of Russell's songs?
3. Give two ways in which songs are used in *Blood Brothers*.

EXAM PRACTICE
Look at Mickey and Edward's song that begins 'No kids out on the street today' (Act 1). Relating your ideas to the context, write a paragraph explaining how this song reflects the influence of folk music and/or musical theatre on *Blood Brothers*.

Set and Staging

You must be able to: comment on what the staging of the play tells us about themes and characters.

What are stage directions for?

Stage directions are there to help directors and actors understand how to perform the play. Sometimes they indicate where and when a scene is happening. Sometimes they tell the actors what to do. Brief directions, placed in brackets after a character's name, indicate what the actor is doing while speaking or how he or she should deliver a line.

How should stage directions be written about?

Think about the effect of the stage directions. How do they affect the mood and atmosphere? How do they show what the characters are thinking or feeling?

When writing about a play always remember that it is a script to be performed and can be interpreted differently by different actors and directors. However, because *Blood Brothers* is under copyright, productions are tightly controlled and the stage directions in the text are followed quite closely wherever and whenever you see it. Therefore, the stage directions can be read as descriptions of how the play is performed.

How does Russell describe the set?

In his Production Note, Russell specifies that there should be one set that does not change.

On one side of the stage is a front door indicating Mrs Johnstone's house and on the other Mrs Lyons' house, described as 'semi-permanent'.

Places like the park could be shown by lighting and the classrooms by the introduction of a few desks. However, the dialogue, song and narration clearly indicate where and when each scene takes place.

The set, in keeping with the style of the play, is not **naturalistic**. Russell's non-naturalistic style could be described as **Brechtian**.

What is meant by Brechtian theatre?

During the nineteenth and early twentieth centuries, most theatre tried to imitate real life, with naturalistic sets and acting, reinforced by the convention of the **'fourth wall'**, meaning that there was an invisible barrier between the actors and the audience.

The German writer Bertolt Brecht (1898–1956) led the way in breaking down this barrier, keeping the audience aware that they were watching a play and not real life. Brecht's style influenced the house style of British theatres like the Liverpool Everyman.

In what ways is *Blood Brothers* Brechtian?

Brecht used songs and narration in his plays, as Russell does. The way in which the narrator speaks to the audience breaks the fourth wall.

Brecht's plays were often about moral dilemmas and choices. In *Blood Brothers* Russell presents Mrs Johnstone's choice and asks the audience to judge it.

Russell's use of non-naturalistic techniques – such as having adults play children, the narrator playing various small parts and the way the action moves between times and places – can be seen as Brechtian **alienation**, keeping the audience aware that this is a play and not real life.

Key Quotations to Learn

The whole play should flow along easily and smoothly, with no cumbersome scene changes. (Production Note)

NARRATOR: Then bring her on and come judge for yourselves / How she came to play this part. (Act 1)

MRS JOHNSTONE *hums a few bars of the song, and dances a few steps, as she makes her way to her place of work – MRS LYONS' house. During the dance she acquires a brush, dusters and a mop bucket.* (Act 1)

Summary

- The play was written to be performed on one set without major changes.
- It is intended to be performed in a non-naturalistic way.
- The play's style and staging can be described as Brechtian.

Questions

QUICK TEST
1. Should you quote and comment on stage directions?
2. Which parts of the set are semi-permanent?
3. Name one example of Russell's use of Brechtian 'alienation' techniques.

EXAM PRACTICE
Using at least one of the key quotations, write a paragraph explaining how Russell's staging helps to involve the audience in the story of *Blood Brothers*.

Liverpool in the 1960s

You must be able to: link the events of Act 1 to its setting.

When and where is Act 1 set?

Act 1 is set in Liverpool. Liverpool is not mentioned but the setting is clearly indicated by a few references and the way the characters speak.

The writer is not specific about when the play is set but references made during the play and the assumption that the play ends roughly at the time of its writing (1982) suggest that it starts in about 1960.

What was Liverpool like in the 1960s?

In 1960 Liverpool was the fourth biggest city in the UK.

During the Second World War (1939–45) about 4,000 people had been killed in the Merseyside area by bombing and thousands of properties were damaged. As a result of this, housing conditions for many were bad during the 1950s and 1960s, despite the economy thriving in Liverpool and across the UK.

How is this reflected in the play?

The housing shortage and the way the city council dealt with it are reflected in the climax of Act 1 when the Johnstones and their neighbours are rehoused in a new town.

Mrs Johnstone's situation is not unique to, or typical of, Liverpool at the time. Her poverty is the result of her husband leaving her with a big family to provide for and her reliance on hire purchase. This was a way of buying goods in instalments, similar to current 'rent to buy' purchases. It meant poorer people could get expensive items such as washing machines and fridges but high interest rates often led to increasing debt and the **repossession** of the goods, as happens to Mrs Johnstone.

There are very few specific reference places in Liverpool. The statue of Peter Pan that the children shoot at is in Sefton Park in the south Liverpool suburbs. Peter Pan is a character who never grows up, created by J.M. Barrie, so it could be significant that they are shooting at a **symbol** of everlasting childhood innocence.

The speech of most of the characters gives a sense of the Liverpool accent ('What y' lookin' at?') and regional expressions are used ('Are you soft?'; 'Y' little robbin' get'), which 'place' the action in Liverpool.

The lack of specific references to time and place suggest a desire to give the play a wider application, its themes being universal (almost **mythical**) rather than rooted in one time and place.

Summary

- Act 1 is set in Liverpool in the 1960s.
- The plot reflects the city's housing problems after the war.
- Most of the characters speak with a Liverpool accent and use local expressions.
- Russell avoids specific references to Liverpool to give the play more general appeal.

Questions

QUICK TEST
1. Where is the first act set?
2. What major problem was the city left with after the Second World War?
3. How does the way the characters speak reflect the play's setting?

EXAM PRACTICE

MILKMAN: Listen love, I'm up to here with hard luck stories; you owe me three pounds, seventeen and fourpence an 'either you pay up today, like now, or I'll be forced to cut off your deliveries. (Act 1)

Relating your ideas to the context of time and place, write a paragraph analysing how Russell establishes his setting and Mrs Johnstone's situation in this quotation.

New Towns

You must be able to: link the events of Act 2 to its setting.

Where and when is Act 2 set?

Act 2 takes place in and around a new town near Liverpool. The reference to 'Skelmersdale Lane' at the end of Act 1 indicates that it is based on Skelmersdale, Lancashire.

As the twins age from 14 to over 21 in this act, we can **infer** that it takes place from about 1974 to 1982.

What was Skelmersdale like?

Skelmersdale, a mining village in Lancashire, was developed into a new town in the 1960s. New towns were built across the country to provide good quality housing and a better way of life for working-class families from inner cities.

Skelmersdale delivered improved housing, with many families getting inside bathrooms and gardens for the first time. However, it suffered from a lack of facilities, poor transport links and an unsuccessful street layout.

At first, new factories provided plentiful employment but many of these closed down in the recession of the late 1970s, which hit the North West of England particularly badly. The town suffered from high unemployment, dependency on state benefits and problems such as drug abuse and crime.

How is this reflected in the play?

The song at the end of Act 1 sums up the attitude of most people who moved to the new towns when they were first built. The scene where the Johnstones arrive in the country comically conveys the experience of many city dwellers in a rural environment.

At the beginning of Act 2 Mrs Johnstone sings about how happy she is with her new home, although the optimism is tempered by her reference to Sammy's behaviour, **implying** that the new towns could not change people's nature.

When Mickey leaves school he quickly gets a job, reflecting the experience of most young people at the time. However, the sequence where the workers are sacked and queue up for the dole soon follows. This vividly conveys the way things changed in the late 1970s and early 1980s. Mickey's depression and his involvement in crime are seen as the results of the economic downturn as the dream of the 1960s town planners turns sour.

As in Act 1, Russell does not include specific references to place. Without the reference to 'Skelmersdale Lane', it could be any new town or housing estate. Indeed, there are ways in which it is not like Skelmersdale at all. Mickey and Linda attend a secondary modern school, whereas in the 1970s secondary schools throughout Lancashire were comprehensive. The final scene is set in the town hall, something which Skelmersdale never had.

This lack of accuracy suggests that Russell is not interested in 'rooting' his play in a particular time and place. The place where his characters live is a product of his imagination, loosely based on new towns of the time.

Summary

- Act 2 is set in a new town outside Liverpool.
- New towns were intended to provide good housing and a new life to people from the cities.
- In the 1970s and 1980s economic recession made life difficult in the new towns.
- *Blood Brothers* reflects the experience of people who moved to new towns.

Questions

QUICK TEST
1. Name two ways in which houses in the new towns differed from those in the inner city.
2. What happened in the 1970s to change the lives of people in the North West?
3. Does Act 2 provide an accurate portrayal of life in a new town?

EXAM PRACTICE
   'The young man on the street, Miss Jones,
   He's walkin' round in circles,
   He's old before his time,'
Relating your ideas to historical context, write a paragraph exploring how Russell conveys the disillusion with new towns felt by many in the 1970s.

You must be able to: analyse how Mrs Johnstone is presented in the play.

Who is Mrs Johnstone?

At the beginning of the play she is 25, with seven children. Her husband has left her and she is pregnant. She works as a cleaner for Mrs Lyons.

What is her function in the play?

She is the play's **protagonist**. The story is about the consequences of her decision to give away one of her twins.

Some of her other actions help to create the tragedy, such as her gift of the locket to Edward and her intervention in the final scene.

Her songs give the audience access to her feelings, creating **empathy**. To some extent, Russell undermines this by not giving her a first name and by inviting the audience to judge her.

What is her character?

In the original play she was called simply 'the mother', suggesting that she is an archetypal mother, defined by that role.

She is **nostalgic** about the time before she was a mother and 'we went dancing'. Her references to Marilyn Monroe suggest she longs for a glamorous life, which she knows is a fantasy. She often mentions dancing, which – like Marilyn Monroe – becomes a **motif** in the play.

She is superstitious and **gullible**, believing Mrs Lyons' made-up superstition about twins.

Why does she give away her child?

Her decision comes from a mixture of her financial problems and sympathy for Mrs Lyons.

She is horrified by Mrs Lyons' suggestion that she has 'sold' her baby but ends up taking the money anyway. She could be seen as **mercenary** and unfeeling.

However, her action can also be seen as selfless, giving one of her children a better life, something that Mickey echoes when he cries, 'I could have been him!'

Is she a strong character?

At first she comes across as quite weak. She says that she has spent her whole life 'knowin' I shouldn't', implying that her weakness of character has led to her current situation. She does not have much influence over her children, although she loves them. In Act 1 she is worried about them being taken into care. Sammy is already in trouble with the law.

She begins to show more strength of character in Act 2. She stands up to Mrs Lyons, refusing her money, and tries to stop Mickey shooting Edward.

Key Quotations to Learn

MRS JOHNSTONE: And did y' never hear of the mother, so cruel, / There's a stone in place of her heart? (Act 1)

MRS JOHNSTONE: I've spent all me bleedin' life knowin' I shouldn't. / But I do. (Act 1)

MRS JOHNSTONE: I ... I thought I'd never see him again. I wanted him to have ... a picture of me ... even though he'd never know. (Act 2)

Summary

- Mrs Johnstone is the play's protagonist.
- She is defined by her role as a mother.
- Her motives for giving away her son are complex.
- At first she is a weak character but she gets stronger through the play.

Sample Analysis

In her first song Mrs Johnstone's background and character are introduced to the audience. Her husband's reported use of **clichéd imagery** (the **metaphor** 'deep blue pools' and the **simile** 'as soft as snow') reveal her gullibility and her longing for romance. This impression is confirmed by the comparison to Marilyn Monroe, implying both her longing for a more glamorous life and her possession of the sort of vulnerability associated with the film star.

Questions

QUICK TEST
1. What is Mrs Johnstone's job?
2. Why does she give her child to Mrs Lyons? Give two reasons.
3. How does she show strength of character in Act2?

EXAM PRACTICE
Using at least one of the 'Key Quotations to Learn', write a paragraph explaining how Russell presents Mrs Johnstone as a mother.

Mrs Lyons

You must be able to: analyse how Mrs Lyons is presented in the play.

Who is Mrs Lyons?

Jennifer Lyons is a wealthy woman who employs Mrs Johnstone as a cleaner. She is married but cannot have children.

What is her function in the play?

She can be seen as Mrs Johnstone's **antagonist**. She provides a contrast to Mrs Johnstone. Her desire for a child leads to the inciting incident of Mrs Johnstone giving her one of the twins. Her action in telling Mickey about Linda and Edward leads to the tragic climax.

What is her character?

She speaks in **Standard English**. The way her lines are written suggests she uses **received pronunciation**, in contrast to the Johnstones, so she is clearly middle-class.

She is friendly towards Mrs Johnstone at first, although quite formal, addressing her as 'Mrs Johnstone' or 'Mrs J'. She is persuasive and convinces Mrs Johnstone that she will give her son a good life.

Her desire for a child makes her ruthless, shown by her making Mrs Johnstone swear on the Bible, her invention of the myth about twins (despite her **scepticism** about superstitions) and her sacking of Mrs Johnstone.

She shows real love towards Edward, her 'beautiful, beautiful son'. Both he and Mr Lyons show affection and concern for her.

How does she change?

Her worry that Mrs Johnstone will take back Edward becomes an obsession. She persuades her husband to move to get away from the Johnstones. Mr Lyons and Edward hint that she is having mental health problems.

In Act 2 she starts believing in superstitions and curses Mrs Johnstone after attacking her. Her behaviour becomes irrational and she is referred to by children as a 'mad woman'.

Is she a sympathetic character?

Some people see her as a 'baddie', responsible for the tragedy. In the original version of the play, she kills the twins. One reason for changing the ending was that Russell wanted audiences to have more sympathy for her. Both her longing for a child and her mental breakdown can invoke sympathy.

Although some people feel that she uses her money to force Mrs Johnstone to part with her child, others feel that she is helping the Johnstones and that Mrs Johnstone has a free choice.

Key Quotations to Learn

MRS LYONS: We've been trying for such a long time now ... I wanted to adopt but ... Mr Lyons is ... well he says he wanted his own son, not someone else's. (Act 1)

MRS LYONS (*almost crying*): Edward, Edward, don't. It's ... what I'm doing is only for your own good. It's only because I love you, Edward. (Act 1)

KIDS (*off*): High upon the hill the mad woman lives, (Act 2)

Summary

- Mrs Lyons is Mrs Johnstone's antagonist.
- She longs to have a baby.
- She is persuasive and determined.
- She is terrified that she will lose Edward and becomes mentally ill.

Sample Analysis

When Mrs Lyons hits Edward and tells him that she does not want him 'mixing with boys like that', the audience might assume her comments arise from snobbery, an impression intensified by her use of words like 'filth' and 'horrible'. However, the audience is aware that the real reason for her anger is her **paranoia** about losing him, arising from her desperation to have a child and her intense love for him. This is clearly shown in the stage direction, '*Gently she pulls him to her and cradles him*', which indicates that a strong visual image of how their close relationship should be created on stage.

Questions

QUICK TEST
1. What action of Mrs Lyons leads to the play's tragic climax?
2. How is she the opposite of Mrs Johnstone?
3. What did Russell change about the play to make her more sympathetic?

EXAM PRACTICE
Using at least one of the 'Key Quotations to Learn', write a paragraph explaining how Russell presents Mrs Lyons.

Mickey (Act 1)

You must be able to: analyse how Mickey is presented in Act 1 of the play.

Who is Mickey?

Mickey is one of Mrs Johnstone's twins, the one she keeps.

What is his function in the play?

The play is the story of his life, from birth to death. He represents the working class. He is a victim of society, but his actions and choices hasten the tragedy.

What is his character?

He is outgoing but sensitive, affectionate and loyal to his family and friends.

How does he show his character through his actions?

He is portrayed as a typical working-class child of his time, playing out and enjoying imaginative, active games based on film or television.

He speaks in non-Standard English, the spelling of his lines reflecting his Liverpool accent ('y' comin' out?') and using local **dialect** expressions and constructions, such as 'y' can't say nottin" and 'Sammy's robbed me other gun'.

He admires his older brother Sammy and envies the extra freedom he gets from being two years older, expressing his feelings in 'I wish I was our Sammy'.

Mickey shows that he is superstitious when he worries about failing to cross his fingers while swearing. He then displays his sensitivity – **foreshadowing** his later breakdown – when he gets upset about dying.

He shows sensitivity to others when he notices that, after moving house, his mother is happy.

He is contrasted with Edward; Mickey has more freedom and shows off by swearing, but he is less well-educated.

How do other characters react to Mickey?

Mrs Johnstone allows him less freedom than her other children, apparently because he is the youngest but really because she is worried about her secret coming out. When she learns that he has been seeing Edward, she becomes uncharacteristically strict and angry.

Mrs Lyons banishes him from the house, but her attitude also comes from fear that the secret will be revealed rather than the reason she gives to Edward, based on snobbery.

Edward immediately feels a bond with him and admires him for the ways in which he is different. His feelings towards Mickey are similar to those of Mickey towards Sammy. Their lives are contrasted throughout but their bond is stronger than their differences.

Linda provides friendship and comfort, defending him to the other children and attacking Sammy on his behalf.

Sammy is a bad influence. He involves Mickey in his activities but picks on him.

Key Quotations to Learn

MICKEY: … me Mam says I'm only seven, / But I'm not, I'm nearly eight! (Act 1)

EDWARD: He could swear like a soldier / You would laugh till you died / At the stories he told y' / (Act 1)

LINDA *notices* MICKEY *quietly crying.*

MICKEY: I don't wanna die. (Act 1)

Summary

- Mickey is the twin that Mrs Johnstone keeps.
- He is a typical working-class child.
- He is outgoing and friendly but sensitive.

Sample Analysis

Mickey's character as a 7-year-old is immediately and effectively established in 'I wish I was our Sammy'. The stage directions inform us that the actor should be 'reciting' this long verse speech. The use of verse indicates that it has a similar function to the songs, letting us in on the speaker's thoughts and feelings. The repeated use of the phrase 'our Sammy' betrays Mickey's working-class Liverpool background while at the same time expressing the family's closeness. Mickey breaks the 'fourth wall' by engaging the audience like a friend with the **colloquial** and intimate 'Y'know our Sammy'.

Questions

QUICK TEST
1. How does Mickey show his sensitivity as a child?
2. Which character is a bad influence on Mickey?
3. Why does Mrs Johnstone allow him less freedom than she allows her other children?

EXAM PRACTICE
Using at least one of the 'Key Quotations to Learn', write a paragraph explaining how Russell presents Mickey as a child.

You must be able to: analyse how Mickey is presented in Act 2 of the play.

How does Mickey change in Act 2?

At the beginning of the act, he is very similar to the Mickey of Act 1, although seven years older. As the act progresses he becomes depressed, jealous and angry.

How does he show his character through his actions?

At first he is portrayed as a typical teenager.

At school he shows no interest in learning 'borin" things but is cheeky and rebellious.

He reveals his insecurity about his feelings for Linda, and his desire to be more like Edward. However, he appears happy and easy-going.

As he becomes more confident, he shows his love for Linda. He also shows his loving nature through dialogue with Mrs Johnstone.

When he loses his job he becomes jealous of Edward and pride stops him accepting help from him. Instead, he agrees to do a 'job' for Sammy and ends up in prison. His working-class pride results in his making a poor choice that contributes to the unfolding tragedy.

He emerges from prison depressed and dependent on drugs. His jealousy of Edward increases when he listens to Mrs Lyons. Extremely angry, he goes to find Edward. When Mrs Johnstone tries to intervene he turns his anger onto her.

How do other characters react to Mickey in Act 2?

Mrs Johnstone gently mocks him about Linda. She is concerned about his problems but cannot help him. She compares him to Marilyn Monroe when he becomes dependent on pills. The Marilyn Monroe motif was connected with glamour and female attractiveness but now reminds the audience of the star's darker side and her tragic death.

Mrs Lyons' motive for telling him about Edward and Linda is not clear but seems designed to hurt them all.

Edward instantly renews his friendship and deep bond with Mickey and shows loyalty and sensitivity when encouraging him in his relationship with Linda, even though he himself is in love with her.

Linda provides friendship, comfort and love, but betrays Mickey by becoming close to Edward. Both Edward and Linda try to help Mickey.

Sammy remains a bad influence, uses Mickey and betrays him.

A series of authority figures are shown as unsympathetic toward Mickey and his problems, contributing to his descent into tragedy.

Key Quotations to Learn

MRS JOHNSTONE: … you've not had much of a life with me, have y'?

MICKEY: Don't be stupid, course I have. You're great you are, Mam. (*He gives her a quick kiss.*) (Act 2)

MICKEY: … I wish I could believe in all that blood brother stuff. But I can't, because while no-one was looking I grew up. (Act 2)

MICKEY: Leave me alone, will y'? I can't cope with this. I'm not well. (Act 2)

Summary

- At the start of Act 2 Mickey is a typical boy of 14.
- He renews his deep friendship with Edward and falls in love with Linda.
- After losing his job, he becomes depressed, bitter, jealous and angry.

Sample Analysis

Mickey changes more than any other character. After losing his job, he changes from an outgoing, enthusiastic boy to a bitter, angry young man. Mickey picks up on Edward's rather **archaic** expression 'tilt my hat to the world' to express the difference between them: 'I don't wear a hat that I could tilt at the world'. Edward's light-hearted metaphor becomes a symbol of class difference, making him look foolish and out of touch with reality.

Questions

QUICK TEST
1. How does Mickey demonstrate a rebellious streak?
2. What stops him taking Edward's money?
3. Why does he go after Edward with a gun?

EXAM PRACTICE
Using at least one of the 'Key Quotations to Learn', write a paragraph explaining how Russell presents Mickey in Act 2.

Edward

You must be able to: analyse how Edward is presented in the play.

Who is Edward?

Edward Lyons is Mickey's twin, who is given to Mrs Lyons by Mrs Johnstone.

What is his function in the play?

The play follows Edward's life chronologically. His story develops in parallel with Mickey's, their paths crossing over the years until the final tragedy. He represents the middle-class experience.

What is his character?

As a child he is polite, friendly and inquisitive, although rather naive. He is affectionate, generous and caring. He does not change much as he grows up.

How does he show his character through his actions?

When he meets Mickey aged seven, the contrast is stark. He speaks in Standard English, using rather old-fashioned **slang** such as 'smashing'. He shows generosity and naivety when he offers Mickey a sweet. His reaction to Mickey shows curiosity and excitement about having new experiences.

Although he shows a rebellious streak in defying his mother, he is generally respectful and caring towards his parents. He shows concern about Mrs Lyons' state of mind.

At the start of Act 2 he appears lonely but his renewed friendship with Mickey and Linda sees him returning to the happy state of mind he had in Act 1.

He displays strength of character when he defies the teacher over the locket. He is **articulate** and sensitive, as shown when he expresses his feelings for Linda. This also displays his sense of honour and his loyalty to Mickey.

Later he helps Mickey and Linda to get a new house and finds a job for Mickey. He and Linda become close but, despite Mickey's jealousy, they are not lovers.

How do other character react to Edward?

Mrs Johnstone has an instinctive maternal love for him. She is impressed by his openness and his good manners.

Mrs Lyons loves him intensely but her worry about losing him affects her deeply. Mr Lyons show an easy fatherly affection for him.

Mickey admires him for the ways in which he is different and knows 'all the right words'. Later he becomes jealous of Edward and distant, telling him he doesn't understand his situation and refusing to accept his help.

Linda enjoys his company and looks to him for help and support. They become close though she maintains that she loves Mickey.

Key Quotations to Learn

EDWARD: You know the most smashing things. Will you be my best friend? (Act 1)

MICKEY: My best friend / Always had sweets to share, (He) / Knew every word in the dictionary / He was clean, neat and tidy, (Act 1)

EDWARD: Look ... Come on ... I've got money, plenty of it. I'm back, let's forget about bloody jobs, let's go and get Linda and celebrate. (Act 2)

Summary

- Edward is the twin that Mrs Johnstone gives to Mrs Lyons.
- He is articulate, inquisitive, naive, generous and loyal.
- He is tries to support Mickey but is rejected by him and becomes close to Linda.

Sample Analysis

At the play's climax, Edward's calm **demeanour** contrasts with Mickey's anger. When he tells Mickey that 'Linda and I are just friends', the audience might not believe him but his one word exclamation in response to Mickey's suggestion that he is the father of Linda's child ('Mickey!'), followed by an angry 'No, for God's sake!' suggests genuine shock. His previous presentation as an honest person and Mrs Johnstone's interpretation of his friendship with Linda would convince the audience of his innocence.

Questions

QUICK TEST
1. How is Edward's speech different from Mickey's?
2. Why doesn't he tell Linda that he loves her?
3. How does Edward show his strength of character in Act 2?

EXAM PRACTICE
Using at least one of the 'Key Quotations to Learn', write a paragraph explaining how Russell presents Edward's attitude to Mickey.

You must be able to: analyse how Linda is presented in the play.

Who is Linda?

Linda is Mickey's friend and, later, his girlfriend, then wife.

What is her function in the play?

She falls in love with Mickey. Both boys fall in love with her. She marries Mickey and has his child (Sarah). When she goes to Edward for help, her involvement with him provokes Mickey and leads to the tragic climax of the play.

What is her character?

She caring, protective, determined, brave, outgoing and witty.

How does she show her character through her actions?

In Act 1 she stands up to Sammy and the older children when they pick on Mickey. In Act 2 she again takes Mickey's side, this time against the teacher. She warns Mickey about Sammy, who she describes as 'a soft get', the mild **expletive** showing her contempt for him while downplaying the seriousness of his behaviour.

She comforts Mickey when he worries about dying.

Mickey and Edward include her in their games and she shows she is equal (and perhaps superior) to them when she shoots better than either of them. She helps to create a lighter atmosphere as the three of them are shown having fun together.

At 14 she is romantic and comically determined, embarrassing Mickey with her repeated declarations of love.

After marriage, her role as a wife and lack of money turn her into another unfulfilled working-class woman, like Mrs Johnstone. Also like Mrs Johnstone, she wants something better.

This and her love for Mickey make her go to Edward for help. She shows naivety in not understanding Mickey's jealousy of Edward and she does not explain her feelings for Edward.

How do other characters react to Linda?

In Act 1 Mickey and Edward both enjoy her company and do not see her as different because of her gender.

Mickey is embarrassed by her attention in Act 2 but it is clear that he shares her feelings. Encouraged by Edward, he asks her out and they marry.

Edward tells the audience he loves her through a song but does not tell her of his feelings until she is married to Mickey. He responds generously to her request for help. His feelings of friendship for Mickey become entangled with his romantic feelings for Linda.

Mrs Johnstone is friendly towards her, is happy for her to marry Mickey and sees her relationship with Edward as foolish but innocent and understandable. Linda calls Mrs Johnstone 'Mam', showing their closeness.

Key Quotations to Learn

MICKEY: Come on, I've got Linda with me. She's a girl but she's all right. (Act 1)

LINDA: I don't care who knows. I love you. I love you! (Act 2)

NARRATOR: There's a girl inside the woman / Who's waiting to get free / She's washed a million dishes / She's always making tea. (Act 2)

Summary

- Linda is outgoing, witty, caring and brave.
- She falls in love with Mickey; both Mickey and Edward fall in love with her.
- She asks Edward for help and their relationship leads to the tragic climax.

Sample Analysis

The first time Linda is seen supporting Mickey, her role throughout the play, is when she finds him crying and tells him that he has to die as 'everyone does'. Her language is childish, as she says that he'll meet his 'twinny' when he dies, reflecting her childish acceptance of traditional beliefs about death in contrast to Mickey's emotional response.

Questions

QUICK TEST
1. What action shows Linda's superiority to Mickey and Edward?
2. On what two occasions does she come to Mickey's defence?
3. What does Mrs Johnstone think of Linda's relationship with Edward?

EXAM PRACTICE
Using at least one of the 'Key Quotations to Learn', write a paragraph explaining how Russell presents Linda as an adult.

The Narrator and the Chorus

You must be able to: analyse the roles of the narrator and the chorus in the play.

What is a narrator?

A narrator is a person who tells a story.

What is the narrator's function in the play?

The narrator speaks directly to the audience. At times he helps to move the story on. At other times he comments on the action. His function is similar to that of a chorus in ancient Greek drama.

He also helps to create an atmosphere of impending tragedy with his constant references to Fate and to superstitions.

Sometimes he speaks to the characters on stage, though they do not react to him.

He sometimes plays minor characters, such as the gynaecologist, the milkman and the two teachers, providing humour.

The narrator does not really have a 'character' in the same way as others in the play, just as he does not influence what happens.

He reacts to what is happening, expressing amusement, concern or sorrow. In this way he can be seen as a representative of the audience.

Some people see him as a rather sinister, perhaps supernatural figure because of his references to 'the devil' and his knowledge of the tragedy that is going to happen.

What is a chorus?

In a musical a chorus is a group of people who sing and dance, sometimes backing the main characters.

How does Russell use the chorus in *Blood Brothers*?

Choruses in most musical theatre help to create an atmosphere and a sense of time and place, for example in the scene where the children play games and at the end of Act 1.

Sometimes the chorus helps to move the story on, as in Act 2 when they are made redundant and join the dole queue.

They share the Johnstones' experiences, giving a sense of how common these experiences are.

Occasionally members of the chorus emerge as individual, minor characters, such as Donna Marie. In most productions of the play actors playing parts such as Sammy and Mr Lyons sometimes join the chorus.

Key Quotations to Learn

NARRATOR: An' did you never hear how the Johnstones died, / Never knowing they shared one name, / Till the day they died, when a mother cried / My own dear sons lie slain. (Act 1)

NARRATOR: You know the devil's got your number, / Y' know he gonna find y', (Act 1)

NARRATOR: It was one day in October when the rain came falling down, / And someone said the bogey man was seen around the town. (Act 2)

Summary

- The narrator tells the story and comments on the action.
- He reacts to what is happening and sometimes appears as other characters.
- The chorus helps to create atmosphere and emotion, sometimes moving the story on.

Sample Analysis

On his first appearance the narrator immediately breaks the 'fourth wall' as he steps forward by speaking directly to the audience. This establishes the Brechtian style of the play. He asks the **rhetorical question** 'So did y' hear the story of the Johnstone twins?', engaging the audience with his friendly colloquial tone while stating clearly what the play will be about. The implication that the audience might already know the story and the fact that he speaks in verse make it seem like a folk **ballad**, a song about a well-known, possibly true story.

Questions

QUICK TEST
1. What does 'narrator' mean?
2. Name two small parts played by the narrator.
3. Give an example of an experience that the chorus shares with the Johnstone family.

EXAM PRACTICE
Using at least one of the 'Key Quotations to Learn', write a paragraph explaining how Russell uses the narrator in *Blood Brothers*.

Sammy and Mr Lyons

You must be able to: analyse how Sammy and Mr Lyons are presented in the play.

Who is Sammy?

Sammy is Mickey's older brother, the seventh of Mrs Johnstone's children.

What is his character?

Because he is older, Mickey looks up to him but he is a poor role model.

Mickey's description of him in 'I wish I was our Sammy' paints him as a typical boy who gets up to mischief. However, he is already breaking the law at the age of 9, stealing from Linda's mother. His behaviour gets worse throughout the play. He is violent but cowardly.

Mickey tells Edward that Sammy has a 'plate' in his head as a result of an accident, giving a hint that his behaviour could be linked to some form of brain damage.

How does he show his character through his actions?

In Act 1 he leads the way in making Mickey cry but backs down when Linda confronts him.

In Act 2 we are told that he burned the school down and we see him stealing from the bus conductor.

He shows that he has influence over Mickey by getting him involved in an armed robbery. Afterwards, he runs away and lets Mickey take the blame.

He represents one possible result of poverty and lack of opportunity, moving from the working classes to the criminal classes.

Who is Mr Lyons?

Richard Lyons is the husband of Mrs Lyons. He thinks that Edward is his son.

What is his character?

He is a stereotypical middle-class businessman. His priority is work and he sees childcare as his wife's role. However, although he is impatient and rather insensitive, he is concerned about his wife's health.

He shows affection towards Edward but their relationship comes across as rather old-fashioned, almost **anachronistic** (for example, calling him 'old chap').

How does he show his character through his actions?

He is first seen playing with Edward, giving an impression of a close, happy family, but he quickly leaves to go to work.

He argues with Mrs Lyons about moving, while showing concern about her health. He agrees to move after being visited by the policeman.

In Act 2 he appears in the factory, making workers redundant. He is used as a representative of uncaring capitalism.

Key Quotations to Learn

MICKEY: I wish I was our Sammy / Our Sammy's nearly ten. (Act 1)

MR LYONS: Jennifer! Jennifer, how many times … the factory is here, my work is here. (Act 1)

SAMMY: … we need is someone to keep the eye for us. Look at y' Mickey. What have y' got? / Nothin', like me Mam. (Act 2)

Summary

- Sammy is Mickey's older brother and a bad influence on him.
- He gets Mickey involved in an armed robbery and lets him take the blame.
- Mr Lyons cares for Edward and Mrs Lyons but focuses on his work.

Sample Analysis

Mr Lyons' traditional relationship to his wife and child is demonstrated by his irritation at Mrs Lyons bringing him home from work, responding to her distress with a curt 'for God's sake, Jennifer' and dismissing her fears. His mild swearing and pointed use of her name make it clear that he is exasperated by his wife's actions. His suggestion that she should take 'something for your nerves' is a heartless throwaway line which, nevertheless, draws attention to Mrs Lyons' increasingly fragile mental state.

Questions

QUICK TEST
1. What crime does Sammy commit in Act 1?
2. Who takes the blame for the armed robbery?
3. What does Mr Lyons do in Act 2?

EXAM PRACTICE
Using at least one of the 'Key Quotations to Learn', write a paragraph explaining how Russell presents the character of Sammy.

Social Class

You must be able to: understand the concept of social class and how it is explored in the play.

What is social class?

Social class is a way of grouping people in society according to how wealthy they are and their social status.

Traditionally the upper classes are wealthy, own land and inherited property and have titles (Dukes, Earls, Baronets etc.).

The term 'middle classes' covers a wide range of people, including people who run businesses, those who practise a profession (lawyers, doctors, teachers etc.) and office workers.

The working class consists of those who do manual labour, whether skilled or unskilled; they do not usually earn as much as middle-class people.

There has always been movement between social classes and recently class distinctions have become less clear, partly because the nature of work has changed and partly because the terms are used vaguely. For example, some wealthy and successful people describe themselves as 'working class'.

How is social class depicted in the play?

Ideas about class are presented in a very simple way. The Johnstones are working-class and the Lyonses middle-class. Each family is portrayed in a stereotypical way.

Mrs Johnstone does unskilled manual work, as does Mickey before he becomes unemployed. They are poor and live in a council house. Mr Lyons is a manager in a factory. The Lyonses own a big house and send Edward to private boarding school, from where he goes to university.

There is a big difference in their experience of family life and their level of education.

How does class affect the characters?

The boys have the same biological parents but very different childhoods.

This relates to ideas of nature vs **nurture**, the debate about whether people's characters are formed by their inherited genetic make-up or their early experiences.

It is clear that Edward's upbringing gives him huge advantages. It is possible that some of this is because of the extra attention he gets, but most of it comes down to money. The Lyonses' wealth means they can give him opportunities in life.

Social class is seen in *Blood Brothers* as fixed, with nobody moving from one class to another. Working-class characters are trapped by poverty and lack of opportunity.

Key Quotations to Learn

MRS JOHNSTONE: If my child was raised / In a palace like this one. / (He) wouldn't have to worry where / His next meal was comin' from. (Act 1)

SAMMY: He's a friggin' poshy. (Act 1)

NARRATOR: Or could it be what we, the English, have come to know as class? (Act 2)

Summary

- The Johnstone family is working-class and the Lyons family is middle-class.
- The twins' lives are shaped by nurture, not nature.
- In *Blood Brothers* people are trapped in their class.

Sample Analysis

While Mrs Lyons sings about her imagined future with a child, Mrs Johnstone is described in the stage directions as 'looking up in awe at the comparative opulence and ease of the place'. The noun 'opulence' suggests wealth of an almost fairy tale-like scale, indicating how Mrs Johnstone should react to her surroundings, which – given the non-naturalistic staging – the audience cannot see. This idea is taken up when Mrs Lyons describes the house as a 'palace'.

Questions

QUICK TEST
1. What sort of school does Edward attend?
2. Which is more important in shaping the twins' lives: nature or nurture?
3. Does anyone in *Blood Brothers* move between classes?

EXAM PRACTICE
Using at least one of the 'Key Quotations to Learn', write a paragraph analysing how Russell presents the advantages Edward derives from his middle-class upbringing.

Fate and Superstition

You must be able to: analyse how ideas about fate and superstition are presented in the play.

What is meant by 'fate'?

'Fate' refers to the idea that the future is mapped out or predetermined.

How is fate presented in *Blood Brothers*?

By showing the end of the story at the beginning of the play, Russell suggests that the twins' deaths are inevitable.

Throughout the play the narrator creates a sense that something bad is bound to happen with his repetition of 'the devil's got your number', using the devil as a **personification** of evil.

What is superstition?

Superstition refers to an irrational belief in or fear of the supernatural, and especially to practices which are meant to ward off evil.

What superstitions feature in the play?

Near the start of the play Mrs Johnstone tells Mrs Lyons that it is bad luck to leave new shoes on a table because 'you never know what'll happen', the expression acquiring significance from the audience's knowledge of what will happen. This shows Mrs Lyons that she can make use of Mrs Johnstone's superstitious nature, which she does by making her swear on the Bible and inventing a superstition of her own about twins being separated.

As the play progresses, Mrs Lyons becomes superstitious as her mental health deteriorates, cursing Mrs Johnstone and calling her a 'witch'.

Other superstitions mentioned include breaking glass, spilling salt and seeing a single magpie. Some of these are mentioned by the children and are a harmless part of their games but they all refer to bad luck. When the narrator sings about them they become more sinister, adding to a sense of impending doom.

There are a few references to religion (the Bible, rosaries, the devil), which are treated similarly to superstitions.

Why are fate and superstition important in the play?

At the end of the play the narrator asks whether superstition might be to blame for what has happened. It is not clear what he means by this but he could be suggesting that irrational ideas have taken hold of the characters and so led to the tragedy.

While the use of superstitions strengthens the idea that the tragedy is inevitable, the overwhelming impression is that it is the result of the society that the characters inhabit and the choices they make.

Key Quotations to Learn

NARRATOR (*singing*): Shoes on the table / An' a spider's been killed. / Someone's broke the lookin' glass / A full moon's shinin' / An' the salt's been spilled. (Act 1)

MRS LYONS: There's no such thing as a bogey man. It's a – a superstition (Act 1)

NARRATOR: And do we blame superstition for what came to pass? (Act 2)

Summary

- The narrator's speeches and songs create a supernatural atmosphere and suggest that the twins are doomed to die.
- Mrs Johnstone is superstitious and Mrs Lyons takes advantage of this.
- Mrs Lyons does not believe in superstitions at first but becomes haunted by them.

Sample Analysis

When the narrator sings about 'the devil' he implies the existence of an evil force outside the characters, reflecting traditional Christian beliefs such as those that Mrs Johnstone might hold. However, he makes him sound more like the 'bogey man', mentioned by the children, which Mrs Lyons dismisses as 'the sort of thing a silly mother might say'. The narrator's references to the devil are, therefore, **ambiguous**. Audiences might infer that he is describing a real, supernatural threat or that he is reflecting, and implicitly criticising, the irrational beliefs of the characters.

Questions

QUICK TEST
1. What does Mrs Johnstone believe about shoes?
2. What does the narrator refer to as a symbol of evil?
3. How might belief in superstition be responsible for the tragedy?

EXAM PRACTICE
Using at least one of the 'Key Quotations to Learn', write a paragraph explaining how Russell presents superstitions in *Blood Brothers*.

Choice

You must be able to: analyse how the theme of choice is presented in the play.

Why is the idea of choice important in *Blood Brothers*?

The characters in Blood Brothers, especially Mrs Johnstone and Mickey, make choices and decisions that lead to the tragedy.

What important choices are made in the play?

Mrs Johnstone's situation is partly of her own making – she was not forced to have children or get into debt.

Mrs Lyons decides to ask Mrs Johnstone to give her a child.

Mrs Johnstone chooses to enter into a bargain with her to do so.

Mickey and Edward choose to defy their mothers and play with each other.

Mrs Johnstone chooses to give the locket to Edward.

Mr and Mrs Lyons decide to move to the country.

Mickey decides not to take Edward's money, preferring to do a 'job' for Sammy.

Linda chooses to go to Edward for help.

Mrs Lyons decides to tell Mickey about Linda and Edward.

Are these choices freely made?

Audiences are usually sympathetic to the characters making the fateful choice, either because of the characters' personalities or because of the situations they are in.

Mrs Johnstone admits to weakness but is also a product of her class and her time.

Mrs Lyons is under pressure to have a child, whether from herself, her husband or society in general.

It is mainly poverty that causes Mrs Johnstone to give away Edward, though Mrs Lyons puts pressure on her.

To Mickey and Edward the ban on their friendship seems irrational and unfair.

Mrs Johnstone cannot resist her natural maternal feelings for Edward.

Mr and Mrs Lyons do not know that the Johnstones will also move.

Mickey refuses Edward's help because of his pride, which many find understandable. This and his poverty force him into crime.

Linda's actions are driven by love. She does not foresee Mickey's reaction.

Mrs Lyons has lost control and does not think about the consequences of her actions.

However, the characters do have choices and tend to make choices that have bad outcomes.

Think about to what extent they create their own tragedy.

Key Quotations to Learn

MRS JOHNSTONE: Yeh, but I don't know if I wanna give one away. (Act 1)

MICKEY: Well, my mum says I haven't to play with you. But take no notice of mothers. (Act 1)

MRS JOHNSTONE: They just said 'hello'. / And foolishly gazed, / They should have gone / Their separate ways. (Act 2)

Summary

- Characters make important choices throughout the play that lead to the tragedy.
- Mrs Johnstone and Mickey's choices are often driven by poverty.
- Characters are often not aware of the possible consequences of their decisions.

Sample Analysis

Mickey's decision to refuse Edward's money in Act 2 mirrors Mrs Johnstone's refusal of Mrs Lyons' offer of money. Both their choices might appear to be principled assertions of independence. Mrs Johnstone is proud that she has 'made a life out here', the word 'made' indicating that she feels in control of her life at last. Mickey's decision is also motivated by pride but is sparked by Edward's lack of understanding of his situation. Immediately after refusing Edward's money, he agrees to commit a crime in exchange for £50, a choice which represents an important turning point in the play and has fatal consequences.

Questions

QUICK TEST
1. How do Mickey and Edward defy their mothers?
2. In what way is Mrs Johnstone's decision to give up a baby not a free choice?
3. What do Mr and Mrs Lyons decide to do at the end of Act 1?

EXAM PRACTICE
Using at least one of the 'Key Quotations to Learn', write a paragraph explaining how ideas about choice and free will are presented in *Blood Brothers*.

Motherhood and Women's Roles

You must be able to: analyse how ideas about motherhood are presented in the play.

Why is motherhood important in the play?

Mrs Johnstone and Mrs Lyons are seen primarily as mothers. Their role as mothers is central to the plot.

How are traditional female roles presented in the play?

Mrs Johnstone's role has been to marry young and have children, the traditional role of the working-class woman.

Before her marriage she was interested in dancing, movies and her boyfriend. She does not have any ambitions, except for the fantasy of being like Marilyn Monroe, an iconic object of male desire.

After marriage she has a lot of children in quick succession. When her husband leaves, she gets a traditionally female unskilled manual job.

Mrs Lyons does not work, reflecting the traditional role of the middle-class married woman. However, she cannot fulfil that role properly because she cannot have children.

As a child, Linda, rebels against traditional female roles by joining in with the boys' games and outdoing them. However, as she ages she adopts the traditional role, looking after her husband, child and house.

How are these roles presented in the play?

Although none of the women fight against their roles as wives and mothers, there is a sense of dissatisfaction and unfulfillment. Mrs Johnstone dreams of unobtainable glamour. Mrs Lyons sees fulfilment in motherhood, but her dream is destroyed. Linda seeks escape with Edward.

What sort of mother is Mrs Johnstone?

She loves her children. She gives them things she cannot afford, jokes with them, shows physical affection and is upset at the prospect of losing them.

However, she has very little control of them. 'The Welfare' has threatened to take them away. Sammy had a serious accident when left with his sister, Donna Marie.

What sort of mother is Mrs Lyons?

She loves Edward. She reads to him, teaches him to dance and teases him about girlfriends.

However, she is over-protective because of her fear of losing him, which makes her suspicious and unpredictable, even hitting him at one point.

Key Quotations to Learn

MRS LYONS: Myself, I believe that an adopted child can become one's own. (Act 1)

MRS JOHNSTONE: They say I'm incapable of controllin' the kids I've already got. They say I should put some of them into care. But I won't. I love the bones of every one of them. (Act 1)

MRS JOHNSTONE: ... you've not had much of a life with me, have y'?

MICKEY: Don't be stupid, course I have. You're great, you are, Mam. (Act 2)

Summary

- Mrs Johnstone and Mrs Lyons play traditional female roles as mothers.
- There is a sense that they are unfulfilled and defined by motherhood.
- They both love their children but are unable to protect them.

Sample Analysis

Mrs Lyons expresses her feelings about motherhood when she answers Mrs Johnstone's question about whether she is 'that desperate' to have a baby, by singing about her fantasy. In the tradition of musical theatre, the song enables her to express her feelings in an honest but **emotive** way. She sings in the present tense ('I look out from this window') as if she can see the child of her dreams, only to have it disappear, almost like a ghost: 'I reach out. But as I do. He fades away.' Her short simple sentences, divided by **caesuras**, emphasise the strength of her emotions, evoking sympathy from both Mrs Johnstone and the audience.

Questions

QUICK TEST
1. In what way does Mrs Lyons not fulfil her expected role in life?
2. Who was looking after Sammy when he had an accident?
3. Which mother is overprotective?

EXAM PRACTICE
Using at least one of the 'Key Quotations to Learn', write a paragraph explaining how Russell uses Mrs Johnstone to explore ideas about motherhood in *Blood Brothers*.

Capitalism and Materialism

You must be able to: analyse how ideas about capitalism and materialism are presented in the play.

What is meant by capitalism?

Capitalism is an economic and political system based on the private ownership of property and profit making. Britain, like most modern states, is often described as a capitalist country.

What is meant by materialism?

Materialism means having more interest in material possessions and comfort than in spiritual and moral values.

How are capitalism and materialism presented in *Blood Brothers*?

Mr Lyons is a successful capitalist. He has an important job in the factory, owns a large house and has money to spend. He is shown in Act 2 making workers redundant. This shows what happens when capitalism fails, resulting in an economic recession. The ordinary workers are powerless.

Mrs Lyons is also an employer, paying Mrs Johnstone to clean for her. When she sacks her, she is not concerned about the consequences for Mrs Johnstone. Having money gives her power. She pays Mrs Johnstone for the baby, perhaps suggesting she sees him as a possession.

Mrs Johnstone is materialistic, spending money on 'junk and trash'. She is impressed by Mrs Lyons' house and sees her child's life there in terms of what he will have. She is a victim of capitalism as the companies who sell to her, encouraging her debts, make money out of her. She sings about the baby as if he were something she has bought on the 'never never' (the colloquial term for hire purchase or buying in instalments with high interest rates).

Edward gains power from money. His father's money buys him a good education and he uses his money and influence to help Mickey and Linda.

Both Mrs Lyons and Edward see money as the answer to life's problems. Mrs Johnstone comes to see that it is not and she rejects Mrs Lyons' money in Act 2.

Capitalism is seen to benefit several characters in the short term, but in the end its influence and their materialism are destructive.

Key Quotations to Learn

MRS JOHNSTONE: Only mine until / The time comes round / To pay the bill. (Act 1)

MRS LYONS: Thousands … I'm talking about thousands if you want it. And think what you could do with money like that.

MRS JOHNSTONE: I'd spend it. I'd buy more junk and trash; that's all. I don't want your money. (Act 2)

MR LYONS: Due to the world situation / The shrinking pound, the global slump, / And the price of oil / I'm afraid we must fire you, / We no longer require you. (Act 2)

Summary

- The Lyons family benefits from capitalism, while the Johnstones are victims of it.
- Mrs Johnstone is materialistic, envying Mrs Lyons' possessions.
- The handing over of Edward is compared to the repossession of Mrs Johnstone's catalogue goods.

Sample Analysis

During Act 1 Russell establishes that Mr Lyons works in a factory and attends 'board meetings', drawing attention to the theme of capitalism through his role in industry. In Act 2 he appears only once, described in the stage directions as 'A MANAGING DIRECTOR' but clearly identified in the dialogue. His language is the language of business, using **euphemisms** such as 'circumstances / Quite beyond our control' and 'surplus to requirement' to distance himself from suffering caused by factory closures. This sort of language also helps to place the event in the context of the economic situation in the late 1970s.

Questions

QUICK TEST
1. What is materialism?
2. Who makes workers redundant in Act 2?
3. Who comes to realise that money does not always solve problems?

EXAM PRACTICE
Using at least one of the 'Key Quotations to Learn', write a paragraph explaining how materialism is explored in *Blood Brothers*.

The Individual and the State

You must be able to: analyse how the theme of the individual and the state is presented in the novel.

What is meant by 'the State'?

'The State' refers to a country or the government and administration of a country. 'The Welfare State' refers to the system of social services controlled by the government.

How is the state presented in *Blood Brothers?*

The Johnstones are dependent on the Welfare State, getting help from national and local government. Although the family gets a lot from the state, this is not generally presented in a positive light.

'The Welfare' – a vague phrase which covers both the government departments which give benefits to the poor and the local council's social services, which look after the welfare of children – threatens to remove some of the children.

The children's education is provided by the state, in the form of the secondary modern school that Mickey attends, but it is unsatisfactory and only reinforces their disadvantages.

Sammy, Mickey and the ex-factory workers are 'on the dole', meaning that they are unemployed and receive state benefits. 'The dole' does not help Mickey back to work or keep Sammy from crime.

The justice system and the NHS, both run by the state, are responsible for making Mickey dependent on pills.

One positive aspect of state intervention is the council's rehousing of the Johnstones in the new town in a house owned by the council. However, their hopes of a better life raised by their move prove to be empty.

Throughout the play employees of the state are presented as unsympathetic, although sometimes comic, figures of authority. Examples include the policeman, the judge, the prison doctor and Mickey's teacher

Key Quotations to Learn

MRS JOHNSTONE: But like they say at the Welfare, kids can't live on love alone. (Act 1)

POLICEMAN: Well, there'll be no more bloody warnings from now on. Either you keep them in order, Missis, or it'll be the courts for you, or worse, won't it? (Act 1)

DOLEITES: Unemployment's such a pleasure / These days we call it leisure / It's just another sign / Of the times. (Act 2)

Summary

- The Johnstones are dependent on the state.
- The Welfare State is presented in a negative way.
- There are several unsympathetic characters who represent the authority of the state.

Sample Analysis

Russell's stage directions specify that Mickey and Linda's school is a secondary modern, a type of school which was associated with low expectations. It is *'all boredom and futility'*, suggesting that their education, and by implication state education in general, should be represented on stage as a negative experience. The teacher insults pupils, calling one a ' borin' little turd', using the crude language of the playground in a way that would be considered unacceptable in most schools today, although more likely a source of amusement to pupils in the 1970s. He is also impatient, repeating the colloquial **imperative** 'Shut up. Shut up.' Once again, an individual employed by the state, is presented as **authoritarian** and uncaring.

Questions

QUICK TEST

1. Who owns the Johnstone's house in Act 2?
2. What is meant by being 'on the dole'?
3. Give three examples of authority figures employed by the state.

EXAM PRACTICE

Using at least one of the 'Key Quotations to Learn', write a paragraph explaining how Russell presents ideas about the Welfare State in *Blood Brothers*.

Violence

You must be able to: analyse how the theme of violence is presented in the play.

What kinds of violence are shown in the play?

Most of the violence in the play, including the twins' deaths, is committed using guns. On two occasions Mrs Lyons is violent.

Why are guns important in the play?

Constant references to guns throughout the play, beginning and ending with the twins' deaths, form a powerful motif.

How is gun violence presented?

The use of guns in the 're-enactment' of the twins' violent deaths at the start of the play has great impact visually and **aurally**.

The children's games, the shooting of the statue and the rifle range foreshadow the violent end of the play. These episodes are innocent and harmless, but they keep the themes of guns and violence in the audience's minds, helping to build tension and a sense of impending tragedy.

Guns are associated with Sammy and his influence on Mickey. Mickey takes Sammy's hidden air gun in Act 1, just as he takes the hidden gun in Act 2. Sammy works his way up from playing with toy guns to injuring (and possibly killing) someone with a real gun.

Mickey's use of the gun is ambiguous. He threatens Edward with it but the stage directions say he 'waves it' and it 'explodes', implying he does not deliberately kill him. Perhaps Russell is saying that he is angry and confused but not a violent criminal like Sammy.

Mickey is killed by police officers, reflecting the idea that he is a victim of society.

How are other forms of violence presented?

Mrs Lyons is shown losing control as she hits Edward 'instinctively' in Act 1. Her action shows the stress that her secret had put her under. It may also indicate the beginnings of mental illness, which is further demonstrated when she attacks Mrs Johnstone in Act 2, this time using a knife.

At the beginning of Act 2, Mrs Johnstone jokes about Sammy's arson and how the neighbours 'sometimes fight on Saturday night'. Taken with the neighbour's hope that it will be 'calm an' peaceful around here' when the Johnstones leave their old house, this suggests that a certain level of violence is accepted as the norm by people of the Johnstones' class.

Key Quotations to Learn

MICKEY: ... (*he produces an air pistol*) He thinks no-one knows he's got it. But I know where he hides it. (Act 1)

SAMMY: We don't use the shooters. They're just frighteners. (Act 2)

On the word 'him' he waves at EDWARD *with his gun hand. The gun explodes and blows* EDWARD *apart. He turns to the* COPS *screaming the word 'No' as they open fire and four guns explode, blowing* MICKEY *away.* (Act 2)

Summary

- Guns are a motif throughout the play.
- Mickey uses Sammy's hidden guns in both acts.
- Mrs Lyons acts violently twice, once in each act, showing loss of control.

Sample Analysis

Russell anticipates the fatal shooting at the climax by introducing serious gun violence half way through Act 2, When Sammy threatens the man in the filling station, he says his gun is 'not a toy', reminding the audience of the children's games in Act 1. ' After the shooting, the connection to Act 1 is made **explicit** when the narrator **paraphrases** the children's 'rule' about dying in a game: '... if you counted ten and kept your fingers crossed'. The tragic irony of his lines suggests a final loss of childhood innocence.

Questions

QUICK TEST
1. What sort of gun do the children use to fire at Peter Pan?
2. What does Sammy do with the gun he uses in the robbery?
3. Who shoots Edward?

EXAM PRACTICE
Using at least one of the 'Key Quotations to Learn', write a paragraph explaining how the theme of gun violence is presented in *Blood Brothers*.

You must be able to: analyse how ideas about mental health are presented in the play.

Which characters have mental health issues in the play?

Mrs Lyons and Mickey have problems related to mental health.

How does Russell present Mrs Lyons as having mental health issues?

When Mrs Lyons gets upset about the attention Mrs Johnstone is paying to Edward, Mr Lyons mistakenly (and ironically) attributes her emotional state to post-natal depression. She is clear that she is not depressed.

However her worry about Edward meeting Mickey makes her unpredictable, crying and hitting Edward. Later, Mr Lyons puts her fears down to her 'nerves' and tells her she should see a doctor. He tells Edward they are moving because she is ill and, after the move, Edward asks her if she is 'feeling better'.

In Act 2, when Mrs Lyons sees the locket, Edward asks her if she's ill again. She attacks Mrs Johnstone with a knife. After this the chorus sings about 'the mad woman.'

There is ambiguity about Mrs Lyons' mental state. Audiences could see her behaviour as typical of someone with a mental illness, perhaps resulting from the stress of her situation. On the other hand, they might see the 'illness' as the perception of those around her who do not know the full story.

How does Russell present Mickey's mental health issues?

When Mickey cries about dying in Act 1, it foreshadows his later breakdown.

After his conviction, he cannot stop crying. The prison doctor diagnoses him with depression and puts him on anti-depressant drugs, to which he becomes addicted. When he gives up the pills, he becomes angry and confused.

Mickey's problems are mainly the result of losing his job and feeling useless. However, his earlier crying might hint that he is already fragile, like Marilyn Monroe. His dependence on anti-depressants raises the issue of how depression should be treated, with Linda urging him to stop taking the pills.

Does Sammy have mental health issues?

In Act 1 Edward is fascinated by Mickey's story of Sammy having a 'plate' in his head as a result of an accident. It is possible that Sammy's violent behaviour is linked to that, as a childhood blow to the head can cause brain damage, resulting in unpredictable, sometimes violent, behaviour.

Key Quotations to Learn

MR LYONS: ... Erm, actually Mummy's not been too well lately ... (Act 1)

MRS JOHNSTONE: It seems like jail's sent him off the rails, / Just like Marilyn Monroe / His mind's gone dancing / Can't stop dancing. (Act 2)

MICKEY: That's why I take them. So I can be invisible. (Act 2)

Summary

- Mr Lyons blames Mrs Lyons' fears on her health.
- Mickey suffers from depression after losing his job and being sent to prison.
- Mickey becomes dependent on anti-depressants.

Sample Analysis

When Mrs Lyons loses control and attacks Mrs Johnstone with a knife, Mrs Johnstone reacts by saying 'YOU'RE MAD. YOU'RE MAD.' The use of capital letters in the text implies that the actor should shout these words and the impact of the accusation is increased by repetition.

The stage direction given to Mrs Johnstone, '(*staring at her; knowing*)', suggests that she is speaking the truth as she realises that Mrs Lyons has suffered a breakdown. This idea is confirmed when her antagonist, who in Act 1 was dismissive of superstition, curses Mrs Johnstone and accuses her of being a 'witch'. The former voice of reason has become irrational.

Questions

QUICK TEST
1. How does Mr Lyons explain his wife's emotional state?
2. What is the main symptom of Mickey's depression?
3. Who tries to stop Mickey taking the pills?

EXAM PRACTICE
Using at least one of the 'Key Quotations to Learn', write a paragraph explaining how Mickey's mental illness is presented in *Blood Brothers*.

You must be able to: analyse how growing up is presented in the play.

Why is growing up important in the novel?

The play follows Edward and Mickey from birth to death, focusing on important stages in their lives.

How are ideas about growing up presented in the novel?

We are shown the twins and Linda at the ages of 7, 14 and in early adulthood (from 18 to early 20s).

Their feelings and interests change with age, as do their relationships with each other.

In Act 1 Russell presents a picture of childhood innocence and fun. Humour comes from this nostalgic view of childhood naivety as they learn about each other and the world.

The working-class children have a lot of freedom and grow up playing outside. Middle-class Edward is more protected and spends more time with his parents. The differences between Mickey and Edward are shown comically, for example through Mickey's swearing. Their childish openness means they can overcome differences easily.

The children are mostly unaware of the darker side of life, but it intrudes occasionally, for example when Mickey worries about death. This reminds the audience that their innocence will be short-lived.

At the start of Act 1 the focus is on the concerns of teenagers. The contrast between Mickey's shyness and Linda's bold declarations of love creates **sentimental** comedy, as does the twins' jealousy of each other. Their curiosity about sex is also depicted comically in the dialogue about the pornographic film.

The differences between Edward and Mickey grow with their different experiences of school but they remain essentially innocent and hopeful, although the narrator reminds us that their happiness cannot last.

In the second half of Act 2 their differences become more important. Mickey and Linda grow up quickly. At 18 he is working and she is pregnant. The scene where the wedding and the redundancies at the factory are interwoven shows the impact of the real, adult world. Edward's privileged upbringing means he does not share Mickey's experience and cannot understand it.

The adult world is dark and cannot be avoided. Their attempts to survive in it end in tragedy.

Key Quotations to Learn

MRS JOHNSTONE: When you mention girls, or courting, / He flies into a rage. (Act 2)

NARRATOR: And only if the three of them could stay like that forever. / And only if we could predict no changes in the weather, / And only if we didn't live in life, as well as dreams / And only if we could stop and be forever, just eighteen. (Act 2)

EDWARD: I'm exactly the same age as you, Mickey.

MICKEY: Yeh. But you're still a kid. An' I wish I could be as well Eddie. (Act 2)

Summary

- The children's innocence and openness creates humour.
- As they grow up their relationships change.
- In the end they cannot avoid the reality of adulthood.

Sample Analysis

The twins and Linda are shown ageing from 15 to 18 in a series of brief images of stereotypical teenage fun, captured on camera by the narrator, who comments on their life in a song. He uses adjectives such as 'young, free and innocent' to describe them, comparing them in a metaphor to 'the lambs in Spring'. This is a powerful symbol of innocence but the reference to the 'fate the later seasons bring' introduces a darker, more realistic note. Lambs live only a few months before being slaughtered. The twins, like the lambs, can do nothing to avoid death.

Questions

QUICK TEST
1. How old are Mickey and Edward when they first meet?
2. Who tells the audience that the characters' youthful happiness will be short-lived?
3. How do Mickey and Edward's circumstances differ at 18?

EXAM PRACTICE
Using at least one of the 'Key Quotations to Learn', write a paragraph explaining how Russell writes about teenagers in *Blood Brothers*.

Tips and Assessment Objectives

You must be able to: understand how to approach the exam question and meet the requirements of the mark scheme.

Quick tips

- You will get a choice of two questions. Do the one that best matches your knowledge, the quotations you have learned and the things you have revised.

- Make sure you know what the question is asking you. Underline key words and pay attention to the bullet point prompts that come with the question.

- You should spend about 45 minutes in total on your *Blood Brothers* response. Allow yourself 5 minutes to plan your answer so there is some structure to your essay, leaving 40 minutes to write the essay.

- All your paragraphs should contain a clear idea, a relevant reference to the play (ideally a quotation) and analysis of how Russell conveys this idea. Whenever possible, you should link your comments to the play's context.

- It can sometimes help, after each paragraph, to quickly re-read the question to keep yourself focused on the exam task.

- Keep your writing concise. If you waste time 'waffling' you won't be able to include the full range of analysis and understanding that the mark scheme requires.

- It is a good idea to remember what the mark scheme is asking of you.

AO1: Understand and respond to the play (12 marks)

This is all about coming up with a range of points that match the question, supporting your ideas with references from the play and writing your essay in a mature, academic style.

Lower	Middle	Upper
The essay has some good ideas that are mostly relevant. Some quotations and references are used to support the ideas.	A clear essay that always focuses on the exam question. Quotations and references support ideas effectively. The response refers to different points in the play.	A convincing, well-structured essay that answers the question fully. Quotations and references are well-chosen and integrated into sentences. The response covers the whole play (not everything, but ideas from throughout the play rather than just focusing on one or two sections).

AO2: Analyse effects of Russell's language, form and structure (12 marks)

You need to comment on how specific words, language techniques, sentence structures, stage directions and the narrative structure help Russell to get his ideas across to the audience. This could be something about a character or a larger idea that he explores through the play. To achieve this, you will need to have learned appropriate quotations to analyse.

Lower	Middle	Upper
Identification of some different methods used by Russell to convey meaning. Some subject terminology.	Explanation of Russell's different methods. Clear understanding of the effects of these methods. Accurate use of subject terminology.	Analysis of the full range of Russell's methods. Thorough exploration of the effects of these methods. Accurate range of subject terminology.

AO3: Understand the relationship between the play and its contexts (6 marks)

For this part of the mark scheme, you need to show your understanding of how Russell's ideas relate to the time when he was writing and the genres he wrote in.

Lower	Middle	Upper
Some awareness of how ideas in the play link to its context.	References to relevant aspects of context show a clear understanding.	Exploration is linked to specific aspects of the play's contexts to show a detailed understanding.

AO4: Written accuracy (4 marks)

You need to use accurate vocabulary, expression, punctuation and spelling. Although it's only four marks, this could make the difference between a lower or a higher grade.

Lower	Middle	Upper
Reasonable level of accuracy. Errors do not get in the way of the essay making sense.	Good level of accuracy. Vocabulary and sentence structure help to keep ideas clear.	Consistent high level of accuracy. Vocabulary and sentence structure are used to make ideas clear and precise.

Practice Questions

1. How does Russell use the narrator in *Blood Brothers*?

   Write about:

   - what the narrator does and says
   - the purpose and significance of the narrator.

2. How does Russell write about fate in *Blood Brothers*?

   Write about:

   - what ideas about fate are explored in the play
   - how Russell presents these ideas by the ways he writes.

3. How does Russell use the characters of Edward and Mickey to write about social class in *Blood Brothers*?

   Write about:

   - how Russell presents Edward and Mickey
   - how he uses Edward and Mickey to write about class.

4. Does Mrs Johnstone create her own tragedy in *Blood Brothers* or is she just a victim?

   Write about:

   - what Mrs Johnstone does and what happens to her
   - how Russell writes about what she does and what happens to her.

5. How does Russell present the character of Linda and her relationship with the twins in *Blood Brothers?*

   Write about:

   - the character of Linda and her relationship with Mickey and Edward
   - how Russell presents Linda and her relationship with Mickey and Edward.

6. 'In the end, neither Mrs Johnstone nor Mrs Lyons proves to be a good mother.' Explore how far you agree with this statement.

   Write about:

   - how Russell presents Mrs Johnstone and Mrs Lyons as mothers.
   - in what ways they could be considered 'good' or 'bad' mothers.

7. Explain how Russell presents the theme of violence in *Blood Brothers.*

   Write about:

   - what examples of violence are explored in *Blood Brothers*
   - how Russell presents the theme of violence by the ways he writes.

8. How does Russell use the character of Mickey to explore ideas about the working class in *Blood Brothers*?

   Write about:

   - how Russell presents the character of Mickey
   - how Russell uses the character of Mickey to present ideas about the working class in the play.

9. How does Russell write about superstition in *Blood Brothers*?

   Write about:

   - what superstitions are presented in *Blood Brothers*
   - how Russell writes about these superstitions.

10. How does Russell use the Lyons family to present ideas about social class and privilege in *Blood Brothers*?

    Write about:

    - how Russell writes about the Lyons family
    - how he uses the family to explore social class and privilege.

11. How does Russell present ideas about female roles in society in *Blood Brothers*?

    Write about:

    - examples of women's roles in *Blood Brothers*
    - how Russell presents ideas about women's roles by the ways he writes.

12. Explain how Russell uses songs to explore ideas and feelings in *Blood Brothers*.

    Write about:

    - the songs in Blood Brothers
    - how Russell uses them to explore ideas and feelings.

13. How does Russell explore ideas about mental health in *Blood Brothers*?

    Write about:

    - what ideas about mental health are explored in *Blood Brothers*
    - how Russell explores mental health issues in the play.

14. How does Russell present the character of Mrs Lyons and how she changes in Blood *Brothers*?

    Write about:

    - the character of Mrs Lyons and the ways in which she changes during the play
    - how Russell presents her changing character by the ways he writes.

15. 'In *Blood Brothers* Russell presents a world where individuals are trapped in the class they were born to.' How far do you agree with this statement?

    Write about:

    - ideas about class in *Blood Brothers*
    - how Russell presents these ideas by the ways he writes.

16. How does Russell explore ideas about choice in *Blood Brothers*?

    Write about:

    - ideas about choice explored in *Blood Brothers*
    - how Russell presents these ideas by the ways he writes.

17. How does Russell explore ideas about nature and nurture in *Blood Brothers*?

    Write about:

    - what ideas about nature and nurture are presented in *Blood Brothers*
    - how Russell presents these ideas by the ways he writes.

18. '*Blood Brothers* is about the individual being crushed by society.' To what extent do you agree with this statement?

    Write about:

    - ideas about the individual and society in *Blood Brothers*
    - how Russell presents these ideas by the ways he writes.

Planning a Character Question Response

You must be able to: understand what an exam question is asking you and prepare your response.

How might an exam question on character be phrased?

A typical character question will read like this:

How does Russell present the character of Mrs Lyons and how she changes in *Blood Brothers*?

Write about:

- the character of Mrs Lyons and the ways in which she changes during the play
- how Russell presents her changing character by the ways he writes.

[30 marks + 4 AO4 marks]

How do I work out what to do?

The focus of this question is clear: the character of Mrs Lyons and how she changes.

'How' is an important element of this question.

For AO1, 'how' shows that you need to display a clear understanding of what Mrs Lyons is like and how she acts, focusing on how she changes during the course of the play.

For AO2, 'how' makes it clear that you need to analyse the different ways in which Russell's use of language, structure and form show the audience what Mrs Lyons is like at different points in the play. Ideally, you should include quotations you have learned but, if necessary, you can make a clear reference to a specific part of the play.

You also need to remember to link your comments to the play's context to achieve your AO3 marks and write accurately to pick up your four AO4 marks for spelling, punctuation and grammar.

How can I plan my essay?

You have approximately 45 minutes to plan and write your essay.

This isn't long but you should spend the first 5 minutes writing a quick plan. This will help you to focus your thoughts and produce a well-structured essay.

Try to come up with five or six ideas. Each of these ideas can then be written up as a paragraph.

You can plan in whatever way you find most useful. Some students like to just make a quick list of points and then re-number them into a logical order. Spider diagrams are particularly popular: look at the example on the page opposite.

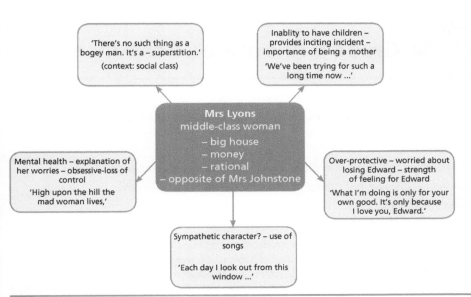

'There's no such thing as a bogey man. It's a – superstition.'
(context: social class)

Inablity to have children – provides inciting incident – importance of being a mother
'We've been trying for such a long time now ...'

Mrs Lyons
middle-class woman
– big house
– money
– rational
– opposite of Mrs Johnstone

Mental health – explanation of her worries – obsessive-loss of control
'High upon the hill the mad woman lives,'

Over-protective – worried about losing Edward – strength of feeling for Edward
'What I'm doing is only for your own good. It's only because I love you, Edward.'

Sympathetic character? – use of songs
'Each day I look out from this window ...'

Summary

- Make sure you know what the focus of the essay is.
- Remember to analyse how Russell conveys his ideas.
- Relate your ideas to the play's social and historical context.

Questions

QUICK TEST
1. What key skills do you need to show in your answer?
2. What are the benefits of quickly planning your essay?
3. Why is it better to have learned quotations for the exam?

EXAM PRACTICE
Plan a response to the follow exam question:
How does Russell use the character of Mickey to explore ideas about the working class in *Blood Brothers*?
Write about:
- how Russell presents the character of Mickey
- how Russell uses the character of Mickey to present ideas about the working class in the play.

[30 marks + 4 AO4 marks]

Grade 5 Annotated Response

How does Russell present the character of Mrs Lyons and how she changes in *Blood Brothers*?

Write about:

- the character of Mrs Lyons and the ways in which she changes during the play
- how Russell presents her changing character by the ways he writes.

[30 marks + 4 AO4 marks]

At the beginning of the play Mrs Lyons is introduced as a middle-class woman who employs Mrs Johnstone as a cleaner. Her house is described as 'opulent', showing she has a lot of money. She also has a husband and no children, so she is the opposite of Mrs Johnstone. (1) Another way in which they are opposites is that Mrs Lyons is not superstitious. She tells Edward that 'There's no such thing as a bogey man.' (2)

The plot starts because she cannot have children and desperately wants them: 'We've been trying for such a long time now.' So when Mrs Johnstone tells her she is having twins and is worried about not coping, Mrs Lyons offers to take one. (3) Mrs Lyons is typical of a woman of her class at the time, who probably would not have a job and whose main role is that of a wife and mother, so she sees having a child as the point of her life. (4)

When she gets the child she begins to change. Seeing Mrs Johnstone cooing over him makes her worried so she sacks her and offers her money to stay away and then makes her swear on the Bible. (5) This shows she is quite cold and determined to get own way. She thinks money is the answer to everything. On the other hand, she does seem to love Edward. She is over-protective and gets angry, hitting him. (6) She calls Mickey 'filth' and 'horrible', the insulting words showing she is a snob. But she calls Edward 'my beautiful, beautiful son'. The repetition of the adjective shows the strength of her love and the phrase 'my son' shows she is possessive and really wants him to be hers. (7)

When she hits Edward it could be the start of her losing control and having health problems. (8) Mr Lyons thinks she is ill, perhaps because of post-natal depression. She says she is not but goes along with it because she cannot tell him why she is 'frightened'. Edward refers a few times to her being 'ill', so the stress might have made her mentally ill. (9) She finally loses control completely and attacks Mrs Lyons with a knife. She curses her and calls her a witch. This shows a big change because in Act 1 she did not believe in superstitions and now she does. Mrs Lyons calls her 'mad' and the kids sing about 'the mad woman' who lives 'high on the hill'. This language is negative and lacks sympathy. (10)

Mrs Lyons' character has changed dramatically because of the bargain she made with Mrs Johnstone. She started out sensible and not very emotional and ends up 'mad'. (11) The audience often finds her very unsympathetic but her actions all come from her desire to have a child and her love for the child. It is interesting that Russell changed the ending from his original play where Mrs Johnstone kills the twins. He did not want the audience to hate her too much but to understand her and sympathise with her. (12).

1. A clear statement, focused on the question, supported by a short embedded quotation. AO1

2. Another relevant point clearly made, supported by a quotation. AO1

3. Clear understanding of the play's structure and its effect. Accurate use of terminology 'plot'. AO2

4. Reference to a relevant aspect of social/historical context. AO3

5. Paragraph begins with clear focus on the question. Examples from text given but it reads too much like 'story telling'. AO1

6. Relevant points made, but underdeveloped and rather muddled. AO1

7. Relevant quotations used effectively. Language analysed using appropriate subject terminology 'repetition'; 'adjective'; 'phrase'. AO1/AO2

8. Introduction of idea about mental illness and loss of control, effectively linked to previous paragraph. AO1/AO4

9. Development of ideas about mental illness, using relevant embedded quotations. AO1

10. Focus on question 'change' and reference back to first paragraph. Attempt to comment on language, not completely successful but showing understanding of effects. AO1/AO2

11. A clear point, focused on the question. AO1

12. Relevant exploration of character's motive and the effect of Russell's methods, related to context. AO1/AO2/AO3

 Questions

EXAM PRACTICE
Choose a paragraph of this essay. Read it through a few times then try to rewrite and improve it. You might:
- improve the sophistication of the language or the clarity of expression
- replace a reference with a quotation or use a better quotation, ensuring quotations are embedded in the sentence
- provide more detailed, or a wider range of, analysis
- use more subject terminology
- link some context to the analysis more effectively.

Grade 7+ Annotated Response

A proportion of the best top-band answers will be awarded Grade 8 or Grade 9. To achieve this, you should aim for a sophisticated response that displays flair and originality. The answer given on these pages to the question on page 64 would meet these requirements.

Mrs Lyons is Mrs Johnstone's antagonist and her opposite. Unlike Mrs Johnstone, she uses Standard English, establishing her as middle-class. (1) Unlike Mrs Johnstone, Mrs Lyons is not superstitious. She laughs at Mrs Johnstone's reaction to her putting shoes on the table and later tells Edward that 'There's no such thing as a bogey man.' (2) She might appear cold and calculating when she uses her knowledge of Mrs Johnstone's superstitious nature to seal their 'bargain', even inventing a superstition about 'twins, secretly parted' to frighten her. Her other weapon is her wealth, which she uses to pay off Mrs Johnstone, successfully in Act 1 and unsuccessfully in Act 2. (3)

However, the most important difference between the women is that Mrs Lyons cannot have children and desperately wants them after 'trying for such a long time'. Her offer to take one of the twins provides the plot's inciting incident: her life will change for ever but not in the way she expects. (4) Mrs Lyons is a stereotypical middle-class woman of the time, whose role in life is to be a wife and mother, making her childlessness of huge importance. Its effect on her is expressed in the song 'Each day I look out of the window', which, in the tradition of musical theatre, shows her true emotions, eliciting sympathy from both Mrs Johnstone and the audience. (5)

*She begins to change after she gets the child. Her reaction to seeing Mrs Johnstone with the child, 'cooing and cuddling as if she were his mother', betrays her insecurity and fear that Mrs Johnstone will reclaim the baby. This **dramatic irony** is continued when Mr Lyons attributes her mood to post-natal depression. (6) When Edward meets Mickey, her reaction is ambiguous. Her anger as she describes Mickey using the pejorative terms 'filth' and 'horrible' betrays her snobbery but also expresses her intense love for Edward, whom she calls 'my beautiful, beautiful son'. The repeated adjective shows the strength of her love, while the use of the possessive pronoun in 'my son' shows how much she wants him to be hers. This scene too is full of dramatic irony, as the audience, unlike Edward, is aware that the real reason for her over-protectiveness is her renewed fear of losing him. (7)*

Her behaviour here, especially her violence towards Edward, marks a change in her character. When she begs her husband to move she cannot tell him why she is 'frightened', so it is natural for him to conclude that 'Mummy's not been too well'. The audience might wonder whether she is just going along with this idea to keep her secret, but after Mickey and Edward renew their friendship in Act 2 there is little doubt that she is ill. (8) Her loss of control is dramatically illustrated when she attacks Mrs Johnstone, the contrast with her former rational self shown by her use of the language of superstition as she puts a 'curse' on the 'witch'. Mrs Johnstone calls her 'mad'. This brutal and unsympathetic description is taken up by the 'kids' who sing about 'the mad woman'. (9) Mrs Lyons' final, silent appearance, as she is seen telling Mickey about Linda and Edward, makes her appear cold and calculating, recalling the Mrs Lyons who did the deal with Mrs Johnstone in Act 1. However, what she does here is irrational and can only lead to tragedy. Destroyed by her secret, she is now almost ghost-like. (10)

In Russell's earlier version of the play, where she kills the twins, Mrs Lyons comes across as the villain of the piece. However, the changed ending suggests a desire for his audience to sympathise with her. The seeds of such sympathy are sown at the beginning when she sings of her imagined child. Some of her later actions might alienate the audience but it is clear that they come from a deep love for 'her' child and that ultimately she is as much a victim of 'the reckoning' as Mrs Johnstone and the twins. (11)

1. A clear statement, addressing the question, using accurate subject terminology. AO1/AO2

2. Considers another aspect of the character, linked to previous point and supported by references to the text. AO1

3. Develops the point about superstition, showing insight and referring to different points in the play. AO1

4. Makes another relevant point about character, which is effectively linked to the play's structure, using relevant terminology. AO1/AO2

5. Focus on context, rooted in discussion of the character and analysis of Russell's methods. AO1/AO2/AO3

6. Clear focus on the 'how she changes' part of the question and analysis of the writer's methods, using accurate terminology. AO1/AO2

7. More thoughtful argument and analysis, maintaining focus on the changes in Mrs Lyons and using accurate terminology. AO1/AO2

8. Continues to focus on 'change' and explores another aspect of the character with some insight, using effective textual reference. AO1/AO2/AO3

9. Analysis of the writer's use of language and how it reflects the change in the character. AO1/AO2

10. Showing awareness of dramatic methods, the candidate refers back to an earlier part of the play to consider how and to what extent the character has changed. AO1/AO2

11. Concluding paragraph brings together ideas about Mrs Lyons and how she changes, referring to the play's context and the writer's methods. The candidate has used language accurately and precisely. AO1/AO2/AO3/AO4

Questions

EXAM PRACTICE
Write your response to the exam question on page 64.
Remember to use the plan you have already prepared. [30 marks + 4 AO4 marks]

Planning a Theme Question Response

You must be able to: understand what an exam question is asking you and prepare your response.

How might an exam question on a theme be phrased?

A typical theme question will read like this:

Explain how Russell presents the theme of violence in *Blood Brothers*.

Write about:

- what examples of violence are explored in *Blood Brothers*
- how Russell presents the theme of violence by the ways he writes.

[30 marks + 4 AO4 marks]

How do I work out what to do?

The focus of this question is clear: ideas about violence and death

'What' and 'how' are important elements of this question.

For AO1, 'what' shows that you need to display a clear understanding of the different examples of violence and attitudes towards them presented in the play.

For AO2, 'how' makes it clear that you need to analyse the different ways in which Russell's use of language, structure and form present these ideas. Ideally, you should include quotations you have learned but, if necessary, you can make a clear reference to a specific part of the play.

You also need to remember to link your comments to the play's context to achieve your AO3 marks and write accurately to pick up your four AO4 marks for spelling, punctuation and grammar.

How can I plan my essay?

You have approximately 45 minutes to plan and write your essay.

This isn't long but you should spend the first 5 minutes writing a quick plan. This will help you to focus your thoughts and produce a well-structured essay.

Try to come up with five or six ideas. Each of these ideas can then be written up as a paragraph.

You can plan in whatever way you find most useful. Some students like to just make a quick list of points and then re-number them into a logical order. Spider diagrams are particularly popular: look at the example on the page opposite.

Violent games – toy guns – theme of guns in Act 1 – Peter Pan and policeman

'The whole thing's just a game'

(context: films, social class/place and time)

Mrs Lyons' violence – association with mental health (link to Sammy?)

'MRS LYONS *hits* EDWARD *hard and instinctively.*'

Ideas about violence

Violence in climax – role of guns – Mickey's mental state – violence of the state

'*The gun explodes and blows EDWARD apart.*'

Sammy – interest in guns – arson – robbery – consequences – the law

'We don't *use* the shooters. They're just frighteners.'

(context – social and economic background)

Attitudes to violence – not taken seriously? – part of life (neighbours fighting) – class and the state

'They sometimes fight on Saturday night, But never in the week.' (context – social norms/class)

Summary

- Make sure you know what the focus of the essay is.
- Remember to analyse how ideas are conveyed by Russell.
- Try to relate your ideas to the play's social and historical context.

Questions

QUICK TEST

1. What key skills do you need to show in your answer?
2. What are the benefits of quickly planning your essay?
3. Why is it better to have learned quotations for the exam?

EXAM PRACTICE

Plan a response to the following exam question:

'*Blood Brothers* is about the individual being crushed by society.' To what extent do you agree with this statement?

Write about:

- ideas about the individual and society in *Blood Brothers*
- how Russell presents these ideas by the ways he writes.

[30 marks + 4 AO4 marks]

Grade 5 Annotated Response

Explain how Russell presents the theme of violence in *Blood Brothers.*

Write about:

- what examples of violence are explored in *Blood Brothers*
- how Russell presents the theme of violence by the ways he writes.

[40 marks + 4 AO4 marks]

From the start the audience knows that violence will be important because they see the 're-enactment' of the shooting at the end. (1) They might remember this when the children are playing games based on films, all involving pretend violence. They sing 'The whole thing's just a game' but they live in a violent world and it will not always be 'just a game'. (2) When the children shoot at the statue they use Sammy's air pistol, which is more serious, and they get caught by a policeman. This shows that violence can have consequences. (3)

There is another kind of violence when Mrs Lyons hits Edward 'hard and instinctively'. She is annoyed about him playing with Mickey and worried about her secret coming out. She then cuddles him to show how much she loves him. (4) In the second act she gets more violent and attacks Mrs Johnstone. This is because the stress is making her mentally ill and the audience is shocked because she has changed so much. (5)

The most violent character in the play is Sammy. There is a hint that maybe he also has some mental illness when we are told about the plate in his head. He goes from toy guns to air pistols when he is a child. (6) He gets Mickey to help him in an armed robbery. He tells Mickey the guns are 'only frighteners', the noun suggesting there is no danger, but after he shoots someone the consequences are terrible for the victim and for Mickey, who goes to prison and becomes depressed. (7)

Mickey uses Sammy's gun to kill Edward. He finds it where Sammy has hidden it, the same thing as happened in Act 1 with the air pistol. (8) The climax of the play is very violent. Mickey's violence comes from his anger about Edward and Linda but also his mental state, the result of unemployment and prison, making him a victim of the economic circumstances of the time. (9) It is as if violence is the only way he can fight back but it does not look like he wants to kill Edward as the stage direction just says he 'waves' the gun and it 'explodes'. The police response is more violent with four guns going off, suggesting the state authorities are violent and more to blame than Mickey. (10)

The attitudes to violence shown are confusing. When the children play violent games it just looks like part of growing up. Mrs Johnstone treats Sammy's arson as a joke and talks about the neighbours fighting 'on Saturday night' as part of normal life. However, we are shown the tragic consequences of violence. Overall, I think violence is important in Blood Brothers *because it is used to express how characters are feeling and to build up to the tragic deaths at the end. (11)*

1. The opening sentence focuses on the question in a clear if simple way, showing awareness of the play's structure. AO1/AO2

2. Focus on a particular part of the play, with clear focus on the question, supported by appropriate quotation and showing some awareness of context. AO1/AO3

3. A new point, supported by reference to the text, not developed. AO1

4. Moves on to a different aspect of violence, supported by quotation, but does not do much more than 'tell the story'. AO1

5. Clear explanation with an awareness of the audience and of the play's structure. AO1/AO2

6. A reasonable attempt to connect ideas through the idea of mental health but does not develop into analysis. Expression is clear and accurate but fairly simple. AO1/ AO4

7. Too much like 'story telling' but uses an appropriate embedded quotation and considers the effect of the language. AO1

8. Refers back to Act 1 showing clear understanding of Russell's dramatic methods. AO2

9. This comes closer to analysis as the candidate considers motivation, mentions structure using correct terminology and shows awareness of context. AO1/AO2/AO3

10. Clear explanation, supported by relevant quotation and with some understanding of the significance of the stage directions. AO1/AO2

11. Struggles to reach a conclusion but shows some understanding of how violence is portrayed and the attitudes shown towards it, referring to social context. 'Ambiguous' might have been better than 'confusing' but it is an honest and understandable response. AO1/AO3

Questions

EXAM PRACTICE

Choose a paragraph of this essay. Read it through a few times then try to rewrite and improve it. You might:

- improve the sophistication of the language and the clarity of expression
- replace a reference with a quotation or use a better quotation, ensuring quotations are embedded in the sentence
- provide more detailed, or a wider range of, analysis
- use more subject terminology
- link some context to the analysis more effectively.

Grade 7+ Annotated Response

The fact that the play opens with a 're-enactment' of the violent climax indicates that violence will form an important part of the play. (1) This influences the audience's reaction as the gun motif is presented in the children's games. Although these games involve no actual physical violence, the audience's awareness of what will happen at the end gives them a dark undercurrent, making the sung declaration that 'The whole thing's just a game' dramatically ironic. (2) Later Linda and the boys shoot at the statue of Peter Pan using Sammy's air pistol. This shows an escalation in the seriousness of the violence, although it is still depicted comically. While the policeman suggests that there are consequences to such violence, he is presented as a comic authority figure, to be both mocked and rebelled against. However, the choice of a statue of Peter Pan, J. M. Barrie's 'boy who never grew up', as a 'victim' might foreshadow the loss of childhood innocence. (3)

The only example of physical violence against a person in Act 1 is when Mrs Lyons hits Edward 'hard and instinctively'. This arises from her fear of her secret coming out, although it might initially appear to be the result of her snobbish disapproval of Edward's new friends; she immediately demonstrates her love when she 'gently pulls him to her and cradles him.' (4) Her violence is presented as part of her intense emotional attachment to Edward and of the stress that her actions have caused her. This theme is developed through references made to her being 'ill' and her identification as a 'mad woman' after her attack on Mrs Johnstone. Mrs Lyons' violence is a symptom of her mental and emotional state. (5)

There is a hint that Sammy's violence might also be linked to mental illness in the absurd dialogue about the 'plate in his head', although his behaviour could be seen as the result of general childhood neglect rather than of the specific incident when he fell out of the window. (6) Whatever the reasons, he is violent from the start of the play and inextricably linked to the gun motif. His graduation from toy guns to air pistol to deadly 'shooter' reflects the escalation in the seriousness of violence as the play moves to its climax. When he carries out the armed robbery his threat that 'it's not a toy' recalls the games of Act 1, a reference picked up by the narrator. The fact that the violence is now real and deadly shows that childhood innocence has been lost forever. This important turning point hastens Mickey's decline and, when Sammy hides the gun, plants the seeds for the violent climax. (7)

Mickey's use of Sammy's gun is another chilling reminder of Act 1 where he boasts of knowing where Sammy hides the air pistol. (8) Now the weapon provides him with an outlet for his anger about Edward and Linda, a feeling fuelled by his mental instability, which has been portrayed as the result of unemployment and prison, themselves consequences of the economic and social conditions of the late 1970s. (9) It is as if violence is the only way he can fight back. The climax itself is ambiguous. The stage directions say he 'waves' the gun and it 'explodes', the imprecise verbs implying that his act *is more of a tragic accident than a murder and should be interpreted as such by actors and director. (10) The police response to the shooting represents a final escalation in violence with four guns going off, perhaps symbolising the responsibility of the state and society for tragedy. (11)*

Attitudes to violence in the play are ambiguous. Mrs Johnstone treats Sammy's arson and the neighbours fighting 'on a Saturday night/But never in the week' as jokes, implying that violence is the norm in their social class. In Blood Brothers violent acts provide a way for the characters to express their anger and frustration, whether with each other or with society. They are also of great importance structurally as each violent act witnessed on stage reminds the audience of the opening tableau and builds towards the play's tragic climax. (12)

1. The opening sentence clearly focuses on the question, using accurate subject terminology and showing an awareness of the play's structure. AO1/AO2

2. Focus on a particular part of the play, supported by appropriate quotation, exploring Russell's dramatic methods, using accurate terminology and showing awareness of context. AO1/AO2/AO3

3. A new point, supported by reference to the text, exploring the writer's dramatic methods and showing understanding of context. AO1/AO2/AO3

4. Moves on to a different aspect of violence, supported by quotation. AO1

5. Develops the previous point thoughtfully, relating violence to other themes in the play and showing awareness of Russell's methods. AO1/ AO2

6. Effective link between paragraphs moves to a new point; alternative interpretations given. AO1

7. Clear focus on the question; Russell's methods explored using appropriate terminology. AO1/AO2

8. Moves to new point by referring back to Act 1, showing clear understanding of Russell's dramatic methods. AO2

9. Analysis of the character's motivation, using correct terminology and showing awareness of context. AO1/AO2/AO3

10. Further analysis, supported by relevant quotation, showing understanding of the significance of the stage directions and allowing for different interpretations. AO1/AO2

11. A further, relevant point, showing an understanding of dramatic structure and linked to context. AO1/AO2/AO3

12. Brings together the strands of the essay, referring to context. The essay is coherent, using appropriate and fairly sophisticated vocabulary as well as being technically accurate. AO1/AO2/AO3/AO4

Questions

EXAM PRACTICE
Spend 45 minutes writing an answer to the question on page 70.
Remember to use the plan you have already prepared. [30 marks + 4 AO4 marks]

Glossary

Alienation effect – a dramatic effect, associated with Bertolt Brecht, used to create a sense of critical detachment in the audience.

Ambiguous (*noun* – ambiguity) – having more than one meaning.

Anachronism (*adj.* anachronistic) – something that belongs in a different time.

Anaphora – the repetition of a word or phrase, usually at the beginning of a line or sentence.

Antagonist – the person in a story who opposes the protagonist.

Archaic – old-fashioned, outdated.

Articulate – fluent and clear in speech.

Assonance – repetition of a vowel sound within words.

Aural (*adv.* Aurally) – related to hearing.

Authoritarian – believing in strict obedience to authority.

Ballad – a poem or song telling a popular story.

Brechtian – theatre style associated with the German playwright Bertolt Brecht (1898–1956).

Caesura – a pause on a line of verse, usually denoted by a punctuation mark.

Chorus – in musical theatre a group of people who sing and dance together; in Greek drama a group of actors commenting on the action.

Chronological – ordered according to time.

Cliché (*adj.* cliched) – an over-used phrase or opinion.

Climax – the high point of a story, usually near the end.

Colloquial – conversational or chatty.

Council house – a house owned by a local authority and rented to the occupants (a kind of social housing).

Connotation – an implied meaning or something suggested by association.

Demeanour – outward behaviour.

Dialect – words or phrases particular to a region.

Dialogue – speech between two or more people; conversation.

Diction – choice of vocabulary in conversation.

Dole – a slang term for state benefits given to unemployed people.

Dramatic irony – a situation where the audience knows something that a character or characters do not know.

Ellipsis (…) – punctuation usually indicating something has been left out, also used in dialogue to indicate a pause.

Emotive – creating or describing strong emotions.

Endearment – an expression of affection used when addressing someone.

Empathy – the ability to identify with the experiences of someone else.

Euphemism (*adj.* euphemistic; *adv.* euphemistically) – the use of mild or vague expressions instead of harsh or blunt ones, e.g. saying 'passed away' instead of 'died'.

Expletive – swear word or exclamation.

Explicit – open, obvious (opposite of implicit).

Exposition – the opening part of a novel or play where setting and characters are introduced.

Foreshadow – to anticipate or indicate a future event.

Fourth wall – in theatre, the idea that between the action and the audience there is an invisible wall.

Gullible – easily taken in or fooled.

Image/Imagery – words used to create a picture in the imagination.

Imperative – an order or command.

Imply – to suggest something that is not expressly stated.

Inciting incident – an event that starts off a story.

Infer *(noun inference)* – to deduce something that is not openly stated.

Irony *(adj. ironic)* – when words are used to imply an opposite meaning.

Lyrics – the words of a song.

Melodrama *(adj. melodramatic)* – a form of sensational drama popular in the 19th century, featuring extreme emotions and action.

Mercenary (adjective) – primarily concerned with money.

Metaphor – an image created by writing about something as if it were another thing (for example, 'You are my sunshine.').

Modal verb – a verb that shows the mood or state of another verb, for example 'could' or 'might'.

Motif – an idea or image that is repeated at intervals in a text.

Musical (noun) – a type of play which includes singing and dancing as well as dialogue.

Myth *(adj. mythical)* – a traditional story, usually involving the supernatural and expressing popular ideas.

Naturalistic *(noun naturalism)* – like real life.

Nostalgic *(noun nostalgia)* – longing for the past.

Nurture – bring up, care for.

Paranoia – an abnormal tendency to suspect and mistrust others.

Paraphrase – put into different words.

Personification *(verb personify)* – writing about an idea or object as if it were human.

Protagonist – the main character.

Received pronunciation (RP) – the standard pronunciation of English in Britain, associated with educated or upper-class people (also known as 'the Queen's English' and 'BBC English').

Refrain – a line or group of lines repeated at regular intervals in a song or poem, usually at the end of a stanza or verse.

Repossession – the taking back of something that has not been paid for.

Rhythm – the pattern of sounds, or beats, at regular intervals in verse or song.

Rhetorical question – a question that that the speaker does not expect to be answered.

Scene – a division of a play, usually within an act; a new scene begins when the time or place changes.

Scepticism *(adj. sceptical)* – an inclination to doubt or not believe.

Secondary modern school – a secondary school for less academic students.

Sentimental *(noun sentiment)* – showing or affected by emotion.

Simile – an image created by the comparison of one thing to another, using the words 'like' or 'as'.

Slang – informal language, often local and changing quickly.

Standard English – the variety of English generally accepted as the correct form for writing and formal speech.

Symbol *(adj. symbolic; verb symbolise)* – an object used to represent an idea.

Tableau – a still picture made up of people on stage.

Turning point – a point in a story when things change significantly.

Welfare (the) – a loose term covering state benefits and the people who manage them.

Answers

Answers

Pages 4–5

Quick Test

1. A re-enactment of the end is shown at the beginning.
2. Mrs Johnstone works for Mrs Lyons.
3. Mrs Johnstone puts her hand on the Bible.
4. He has died.

Exam Practice

Answers might include the way the opening changes the audience's interest from what might happen to how and why it will happen, the narrator's invitation to 'judge' the mother; focus on the Johnstones' poverty, contrast between Mrs Lyons and Mrs Johnstone and the narrator's warning about the consequences of their deal.

Analysis might include a discussion of the narrator's rhetorical question, the visual impact of the re-enacted scene, use of rhyme and rhythm, contrast between Mrs Lyons' imperative and the stage direction ('*almost inaudibly*'), Mrs Lyons' use of Mrs Johnstone's superstitious nature and the dramatic irony of her warning about the twins' death.

Pages 6–7

Quick Test

1. They cut their hands and mix their blood.
2. She forbids Edward from seeing Mickey.
3. A locket containing a picture of her and Mickey.
4. She is happy and optimistic.

Exam Practice

Answers might focus on the shock both experience, the way they try to stop the friendship, Mrs Lyons' snobbery, Mrs Johnstone's changing attitude to Edward, her gift of the locket, Mrs Lyons' growing fear and the reaction of her husband, and the 'solution' of moving house.

Analysis might include **connotations** of the phrase 'blood brothers', the dramatic irony of their becoming blood brothers, the way this foreshadows the tragedy, Mrs Johnstone's use of childish superstition ('the bogey man'), her use of imperatives and her use of non-Standard English (in contrast to Mrs Lyons).

Pages 8–9

Quick Test

1. 14.
2. A secondary modern school.
3. He will not give the locket to the teacher.
4. Move away.

Exam Practice

Answers could focus on the boys' interest in each other, their envy of each other, Linda's attraction to Mickey, his shyness about her, their growing interest in sex, the comic treatment of their growing up and a sense of impermanence.

Analysis might include the use of the narrator, his **diction** implying their childishness ('go and play'), their lack of interest in the future, 'the end of the day' as a metaphor reminding the audience of the tragedy to come, and the use of rhyme and rhythm.

Pages 10–11

Quick Test

1. Under the floor in his mother's house.
2. He gets them a house and gets Mickey a job.
3. Mrs Lyons.
4. That he and Edward are brothers.

Exam Practice

Answers could focus on Mickey's mental state, the tension between Mickey and Edward, Mickey's anger, the robbery, Sammy hiding the gun, Mickey's depression, tension between him and Linda, Linda's going to see Edward, Mrs Lyons' meeting with Mickey, reactions of Mrs Johnstone and the chorus, the atmosphere in the town hall and the inevitability of the climax.

Analysis might focus on the audience's awareness of what might happen, the visual/aural contrast between the lonely figure of Mickey and the bells, with connotations of celebration and joy, tension created by the pause in Mickey's line followed by the repetition of 'I could have been', and the release of tension in Mrs Johnstone's reaction.

Pages 12–13

Quick Test

1. With a re-enactment/tableau showing the end.
2. With songs and the narrator's speeches.
3. The audience knows the play will end in tragedy.
4. Mickey shoots Edward and is himself shot.

Exam Practice

Answers might focus on the surprise of opening the play with a preview of the ending, how this changes the way the audience watches the unfolding drama, the dramatic irony of the end of Act 1, the use of song at the beginning of Act 2 to give an exposition of the family's new life, the excitement of the climax and the effect of Mrs Johnstone's reaction.

Analysis might include the impact of seeing the deaths as soon as 'The lights come up', the lack of dialogue at the start, the cheerful tone set by the rhythm and rhyme of 'Oh, bright new day', the dramatic irony of that phrase, the use of the chorus at the end, ambiguity about who is being addressed, the urgency of the imperatives, the use of repetition and the connotations of the references to 'story', 'movie' and 'Marilyn Monroe'.

Pages 14–15

Quick Test

1. *Breezeblock Park* / *John, Paul, George, Ringo ... and Bert* / *Educating Rita*.
2. He spent a lot of time listening to women (as a hairdresser).
3. School children (secondary).
4. The play focuses on growing up/ the themes and plot and quite simple.

Exam Practice

Answers might focus on the influence of Russell's experience of school, the idea that secondary moderns were for 'failures', the contrast with Edward's private school, the content of the lesson being irrelevant, the lack of working-class characters who benefit from education and reference to the original audience for the show (schools).

Analysis might focus on the colloquial dialogue, humour derived from the subject matter, the irony of 'when you can't get a job' and the changing economic context shown when Mickey can get a job but then loses it (his education being irrelevant).

Pages 16–17

Quick Test

1. New songs on local themes.
2. It makes them easy to remember.
3. To express feelings/ to advance the plot/ to link scenes.

Exam Practice

Answers might include the use of the song to express characters' thoughts and emotions, the song as a 'bridge' between scenes, possibly covering a time lapse, the subject matter (ordinary lives) and the use of simple everyday language.

Analysis might focus on the rhyme scheme and how it changes, use of **refrains** and repetition, the change in the music between 'Long Sunday afternoon' and 'my best friend', the use of separate areas of the stage so the boys sing a duet while apart, and the colloquial/childish language.

Pages 18–19

Quick Test

1. Yes.
2. The Lyons and Johnstone homes.
3. Adults playing children/the narrator playing small parts/ the way the action moves between times and places.

Exam Practice

Answers might include the lack of set helping the action to be continuous, the lack of naturalism meaning scenes can take place in a variety of places, the use of songs to advance the action and as bridges between scenes, and the relationship of the narrator to the audience.

Analysis might include how the adverbs 'easily' and 'smoothly' set the style of the play, the narrator's invitation to the audience to judge as an example of Brechtian alienation, the phrase 'play this part' reminding the audience that the play is not real, how Mrs Johnstone's humming and dancing creates a smooth transition between scenes and her acquisition of 'cleaning materials' conveys her relationship to Mrs Lyons.

Pages 20–21

Quick Test

1. Liverpool.
2. A shortage of housing.
3. They speak in Liverpool accents, using local expressions – these features of the writing place the play in Liverpool.

Exam Practice

Answers might include the milkman as someone whose relationship with people is a commercial one, how the scene establishes that Mrs Johnstone owes him money, the sense that a lot of people are in the same situation ('I'm fed up with hard luck stories') and the reference to pre-decimal money reflecting the time the play is set.

Analysis might include his use of the colloquial **endearment** 'love', showing familiarity, his exasperation showing his frustration at not being paid ('I'm up to here') and his apparent reluctance to take action ('I'll be forced to') contrasting with the sense of urgency conveyed in 'today, like now'.

Pages 22–23

Quick Test

1. They had gardens and inside bathrooms.
2. Economic recession and the resulting unemployment.
3. It reflects life in new towns, but not in a particular one.

Exam Practice

Answers might include the optimism reflected in 'Oh, bright new day', Mrs Johnstone's happiness at the beginning of Act 2, hints that the move has not solved all the family's problems (Sammy's criminality and the unsatisfactory education), the sudden change brought about by the factory closures, the effect of unemployment on Mickey and the failure of the new town to improve lives or change society.

Pages 24–25

Quick Test

1. She is a cleaner.
2. Any two of the following: Mrs Johnstone feels sorry for Mrs Lyons/she thinks he will have a better life/she cannot afford to look after him.
3. She refuses Mrs Lyons' money/ she tries to stop Mickey from shooting Edward.

Exam Practice

Answers might focus on her difficulty coping, her decision to give away Edward, her regrets about the decision and reaction to him as a baby, her relationship with Mickey, her scenes with Edward, her lack of influence on Sammy, her concern for Mickey in Act 2 and her final, fateful decision to tell the truth at the end.

Analysis might include her assessment of herself as 'cruel', her image of her heart as a 'stone', the effect of her rhetorical question, the humorous account of her overspending, the possible application of this to her frequent pregnancies, her use of colloquial language and mild expletive, and the sincerity of her explanation of giving the locket to Edward.

Pages 26–27

Quick Test

1. She tells Mickey about Edward and Linda.
2. She is wealthy, middle-class and childless.
3. Unlike in the original, she does not kill the boys.

Exam Practice

Answers might focus on her role and society's expectations, her husband's attitude, the contrast with Mrs Johnstone's many children, how her fantasy of motherhood is expressed in a song about an imagined child, the way she persuades Mrs Johnstone to agree to her plan, her reaction to the baby, her deep love for Edward, her possessiveness and the effect of the intensity of her desire on her character and on the plot.

Analysis might include the use of **ellipsis** as she explains her situation, the contrast with Mrs Johnstone's many children, her emotion ('almost crying') after hitting Edward, her repetition of his name and 'it's only' and how the kids mocking her as 'the mad woman' shows how much she has changed as a result of her desire to have a child.

Pages 28–29

Quick Test

1. He gets upset when the children say he will die and go to hell.
2. Sammy.
3. She is worried about her secret coming out.

Exam Practice

Answers might focus on his presentation as a typical 7-year-old child, his desire for more freedom, his relationships with Sammy and Linda, his childish language, his interest in swearing, his sensitivity, his belief in superstition, the contrast between him and Edward, his cheekiness, the way he disobeys his mother, his openness and the strength of his feelings.

Analysis might focus on his use of the regional 'me Mam', humour derived from the distinction made between being 'only seven' and 'nearly eight', Edward's comparison of him to a 'soldier' suggesting childish admiration, Edward's use of the common metaphor 'laugh till you died' and 'that blood brother stuff' illustrating the contrast between the adult and the child.

Pages 30–31

Quick Test

1. He tells the teacher what he thinks of the lesson.
2. Pride/envy.
3. He thinks Edward is having an affair with Linda.

Exam Practice

Answers could focus on his depiction as a typical 14-year-old, his relationship with his mother, his relationships with Linda and Edward, his experience of school, his experience as typical of a working-class man at the time, his role as victim, the changes in his personality and their causes, his jealousy and anger, and his status as a tragic figure.

Analysis might focus on his use of understatement in his conversation with Mrs Johnstone, the impact of the 'quick kiss' he gives her, his deprecation of the idea of 'blood brothers' in contrast with his childish enthusiasm, his use of the imperative 'leave me alone' and the vague understatement of the expression 'I'm not well.'

Pages 32–33

Quick Test

1. He uses received pronunciation and Standard English.
2. He knows Mickey loves her.
3. He stands up to the teacher about the locket.

Exam Practice

Answers could focus on the difference in class, Edward's admiration for Mickey and envy of his freedom, the symbolism of their becoming 'blood brothers', his generosity towards him, his visit to Mrs Johnstone, his envy of him as a teenager, his sensitivity about Mickey's feelings for Linda, his lack of

Answers

Analysis might include admiration and closeness implied by the repetition of 'our Sammy', his downplaying of the crime to Mickey, his use of Mickey's situation to persuade him, his use of a rhetorical question and his answering of it, and his association of Mickey's situation with Mrs Johnstone's ('like me Mam'), implying that crime is the only way out for people of their class.

understanding of Mickey's situation, his attempts to help Mickey, his relationship with Linda and his final confrontation with Mickey.

Analysis might include his old-fashioned, middle-class slang ('smashing'), his open and direct manner, his use of the phrase 'my best friend' repeated by Mickey in his song, 'sweets to share' foreshadowing Edward's later attempts to help Mickey, Mickey's listing of his qualities, which focuses on ways in which he is his opposite, and the well-meaning but uncomprehending attitude shown in 'I've got money, plenty of it'.

Pages 34–35
Quick Test
1. Hitting the target when she shoots Peter Pan.
2. When Sammy and the children pick on him/ when the teacher shouts at him.
3. She thinks it is harmless and understandable.

Exam Practice

Answers might focus on the change in her status as she becomes a wife and mother, the contrast with her carefree life as a teenager, her attempts to help Mickey, comparisons with Mrs Johnstone, her deception of Edward when she goes to Edward for help and her actions when she realises Mickey has the gun.

Analysis might include her repetition of 'I love you', showing both the strength of her love and her straightforward nature, the expression 'girl inside the woman' suggesting that she has not changed, the sense that she is imprisoned by her role as a woman and the use of everyday examples (washing dishes and making tea) to illustrate how limited her life is.

Pages 36–37
Quick Test
1. Someone who tells a story.
2. The gynaecologist/ the milkman/ Edward's teacher/ Mickey's teacher.
3. Moving house/playing/the wedding.

Exam Practice

Answers might focus on his role as story-teller, how he comments on the action, his role as a 'bridge' between the audience and the action, his use as an alienation technique distancing the action, his playing of small roles, the idea that he might be sinister or supernatural, the way he addresses the characters and his contribution to the play's humour.

Analysis might include how he speaks in verse, the rhyme and rhythm of his speeches resembling that of ballads, his use of rhetorical questions to involve the audience, reference to 'the devil' as a personification of evil, direct address to characters, ambiguity about whether evil is seen as real or he is reflecting the characters' superstition, and his use of the past tense to tell the story.

Pages 38–39
Quick Test
1. He steals from Linda's mother.
2. Mickey.
3. He makes the workers redundant.

Exam Practice

Answers might focus on his violence, his interest in death, the plate in his head, his connection to guns, his relationships with Mrs Johnstone and Mickey, the way he gets Mickey to join him in the robbery, his cowardice and the importance to the plot of his action in hiding the gun.

Pages 40–41
Quick Test
1. A (private) boarding school.
2. Nurture.
3. No.

Exam Practice

Answers might focus on the relative luxury of the Lyons home, the material goods that Mrs Johnstone imagines him having, the attention he gets from his parents, his interest in books and the dictionary, being able to give sweets and a toy gun to Mickey, going to a private school and university, and the apparent ease with which he becomes a councillor.

The connotations of Mrs Johnstone's use of the word 'palace' to describe the Lyons' house, the contrast with the life he would have had not knowing 'where/His next meal was comin' from', Sammy's use of slang and a mild expletive to describe him and the narrator's use of a rhetorical question to lead the audience into thinking about social class.

Pages 42–43
Quick Test
1. New shoes on the table are unlucky.
2. The devil.
3. It might cause people to act irrationally.

Exam Practice

Answers could focus on Mrs Johnstone's belief in superstitions, Mrs Lyons' scepticism, her making use of Mrs Johnstone's superstitions, the narrator's speeches, which list common superstitions, association of superstitions and evil, the change in Mrs Lyons' attitude and the questions raised by the narrator's assertion that superstition could be to blame for the tragedy.

Analysis might include the effect of the narrator's listing of common superstitions associated with bad luck, the dismissive way in which Mrs Lyons talks of the bogey man, the narrator's use of the inclusive pronoun 'we' and his use of a rhetorical question to make the audience think about superstition.

Page 44–45
Quick Test
1. They continue to play together.
2. She is poor/she is worried about the children being taken from her.
3. Move house.

Exam Practice

Answers might focus on Mrs Johnstone giving Mrs Lyons the choice of twin, Mickey and Edward's choice to be friends, Mrs Johnstone's decision to give the locket to Edward, Linda's choice between Mickey and Edward, Mickey's choice of refusing Edward's money and taking Sammy's, Linda's decision to see Edward, Mrs Lyons' telling Mickey about Linda and Edward, and how far any of these choices are freely made.

Analysis might include Mrs Johnstone's hesitation, her use of the phrase 'give one away' rather than 'sell', Mickey's use of reported speech, his use of the imperative ('take no notice'), Mrs Johnstone's downplaying of Edward and Linda's meeting ('they just …'), the **modal verb** 'should' used to imply that a wrong decision has been made and her use of **assonance** ('gazed/ways') helping to create a gentle tone.

Pages 46–47
Quick Test
1. She cannot have children.
2. Donna Marie (his sister).
3. Mrs Lyons.

Exam Practice

Answers might focus on Mrs Johnstone's inability to manage financially, the suggestion that she puts some of her children 'in care', her mothering instincts towards both Edward and Mickey, her conversations with Mickey, her indifference to Sammy's offending, the moral issues surrounding her actions in giving away Edward and her futile attempts to save them at the end.

Analysis might include her repetition of 'they say', indicating her attitude to authority, her revelation through reported speech that there is a problem about 'controllin'' them, her use of the sentimental regional expression 'love the bones', the impact of the short simple declaration 'But I won't', her questioning of her own ability and Mickey's rejection of her doubts in plain colloquial language.

Pages 48–49

Quick Test

1. Over-valuing possessions and comfort.
2. Mr Lyons (the Managing Director).
3. Mrs Johnstone.

Exam Practice

Answers could focus on the effect on Mrs Johnstone of buying things she cannot afford, the role of money in the 'bargain' over the babies, the attraction of the comfort the Lyonses might provide, the impact of unemployment, the impact of Linda's efforts to get a house and the failure of money to solve problems

Analysis might include Mrs Johnstone's use of the language of finance to describe her situation with the twins, the repetition of 'thousands', the use of the nouns 'junk' and 'trash' to show the worthlessness of material goods and the use of a song to connect the characters' financial position to capitalism and economics.

Pages 50–51

Quick Test

1. The local council.
2. Claiming benefits when unemployed.
3. The policeman/the gynaecologist/Mickey's teacher/ the bus conductor/ the judge/ the prison doctor/ the prison warder.

Exam Practice

Answers could focus on 'the Welfare', the gynaecologist, the family being rehoused by the local council, Sammy being on the 'dole', the prison doctor's prescription, the rise in unemployment and consequent dependence on state benefits, and the power of Edward as a councillor to get a house for Mickey and Linda.

Analysis might include the vagueness of the term 'the Welfare', the sense of it as part of a State that interferes in lives, her acknowledgement that love is not enough, the irony of the 'Doleites' verse and the implication that unemployment is not taken seriously but accepted as 'just another sign of the times'.

Pages 52–53

Quick Test

1. An air pistol.
2. He hides it in his mother's house.
3. Mickey.

Exam Practice

Answers might focus on the children's games, Sammy's air pistol, the shooting of Peter Pan, the rifle range, the guns used showing an escalation in violence, the use of a gun in the robbery, the significance of Sammy hiding the guns and the role of guns in the climax.

Analysis might include the air pistol representing an escalation in violence, the hiding of the gun foreshadowing the hiding of the gun in Act 2, Sammy's use of the euphemistic nouns 'shooters' and 'frighteners' to downplay the danger, the ambiguity in the stage directions 'waves' and 'the gun explodes' suggesting that Mickey may not deliberately kill Edward and the impact of the extreme violence at the climax.

Pages 54–55

Quick Test

1. Post-natal depression.
2. Constant crying.
3. Linda.

Exam Practice

Answers might focus on the foreshadowing of his problems when he cries in Act 1, the implication that being out work and imprisonment have caused his depression, the doctor's diagnosis, the way the drugs are seen as making him worse and the fatal effects of coming off the medication.

Analysis might include the use of song to explain his state to the audience, the comparison to Marilyn Monroe, the use of the motif of dancing as a metaphor for his mental state, Mickey's use of a simple sentence and a minor sentence to explain his drug dependency and the impact of the adjective 'invisible' as a metaphor for his feelings.

Pages 56–57

Quick Test

1. 7
2. The narrator.
3. Mickey is working but loses his job; Edward is at university.

Exam Practice

Answers might focus on how the teenage characters are seen as essentially innocent, their enjoyment of life, their openness, their growing interest in sex, their experiences of school and what happens to them after school.

Analysis might include Mrs Johnstone's depiction of Mickey as a typical teenager, the narrator's use of **anaphora** ('and only if') and Mickey's insulting use of the slang word 'kid' to show the differences between his and Edward's experiences.

Pages 60–61

Exam Practice

Use the mark scheme on page 80 to self-assess your strengths and weaknesses. The estimated grade boundaries are included so you can assess your progress towards your target grade.

Pages 62–63

Quick Test

1. Understanding of the whole text, specific analysis and terminology, awareness of the relevance of context, a well-structured essay and accurate writing.
2. Planning focuses your thoughts and allows you to produce a well-structured essay.
3. Quotations give you more opportunities to do specific AO2 analysis.

Exam Practice

Ideas might include: the way he speaks shows his regional and class background; his life is contrasted with Edward's; the portrayal of working-class family life can be seen as sentimental; his lack of education and material goods shows the deprivation of working-class life; the policeman's reaction to him, contrasted with his attitude to Edward, shows the relationship between authority and the working classes; he gets an unskilled manual job, a typical working-class experience of the time; the loss of his job because of economic conditions is also typical; he shows a defiant working-class pride in refusing Edward's money; his lack of opportunity leads him to crime; he is seen as a victim of the class system; he thinks his life would have been better had he been the twin Mrs Lyons chose.

Answers

Exam Practice

Use the mark scheme to self-assess your strengths and weaknesses. Work up from the bottom, putting a tick by things you have fully accomplished, a ½ by skills that are in place but need securing and underlining areas that need particular development. The estimated grade boundaries are included so you can assess your progress towards your target grade.

Pages 68–69

Quick Test

1. Understanding of the whole text, specific analysis and terminology, awareness of the relevance of context, a well-structured essay and accurate writing.
2. Planning focuses your thoughts and allows you to produce a well-structured essay.
3. Quotations give you more opportunities to do specific AO2 analysis.

Exam Practice

Ideas might include: the narrator indicates the main reason for the tragedy is social class; the Johnstones presented as victims; Mrs Johnstone is trapped by poverty and threatened by 'the Welfare'; authority figures as representatives of an oppressive society; Mickey's education prepares him for failure; working-class characters are either doing unfulfilling jobs or are dependent on benefits; Mickey is trapped by his position in society; Mrs Lyons can also be seen as being crushed by the expectations of society.

On the other hand: Mrs Johnstone creates her own problems; she has a choice about whether to give up the baby; the authority figures are trying to help and/or reacting to the behaviour of the Johnstones; Linda and Mickey defy the teacher so cannot be said to be 'crushed'; Mickey's job gives him money and therefore freedom; Mickey contributes to his difficulties by, for example, joining Sammy in the robbery; Mrs Lyons chooses to take the baby and all her problems stem from this choice.

Grade	AO1 (12 marks)	AO2 (12 marks)	AO3 (6 marks)
6–7+	A convincing, well-structured essay that answers the question fully. Quotations and references are well-chosen and integrated into sentences. The response covers the whole play.	Analysis of the full range of Russell's methods. Thorough exploration of the effects of these methods. Accurate range of subject terminology.	Exploration is linked to specific aspects of the play's contexts to show detailed understanding.
4–5	A clear essay that always focuses on the exam question. Quotations and references support ideas effectively. The response refers to different points in the play.	Explanation of Russell's different methods. Clear understanding of the effects of these methods. Accurate use of subject terminology.	References to relevant aspects of context show clear understanding.
2–3	The essay has some good ideas that are mostly relevant. Some quotations and references are used to support the ideas.	Identification of some different methods used by Russell to convey meaning. Some subject terminology.	Some awareness of how ideas in the play link to its context.